POM-QM FOR WINDOWS

VERSION 3

SOFTWARE FOR DECISION SCIENCES:

QUANTITATIVE METHODS, MANAGEMENT SCIENCE, PRODUCTION AND OPERATIONS MANAGEMENT

HOWARD J. WEISS

TEMPLE UNIVERSITY

PEARSON

Prentice Hall

UPPER SADDLE RIVER, NEW JERSEY 07458

Library of Congress Cataloging-in-Publication Data

Weiss, Howard J.
  POM-QM for Windows, version 3 : software for decision sciences : quantitative methods,
management science, production and operations management / Howard J. Weiss.
     p. cm.
  ISBN 0-13-221772-4 (pbk.)
  1. Decision support systems. 2. POM-QM for Windows (Electronic resource) 3. Operations
research--Data processing. 4. Production management--Data processing. I. Title.
  T58.62.W46 2006
  658.4'0340285--dc22

                           2005053522

Acquisitions Editor/Project Manager: Alana Bradley
Editorial Director: Jeff Shelstad
Editorial Assistant: Barbara Witmer
Media Product Development Manager: Nancy Welcher
Executive Marketing Manager: Debbie Clare
Senior Managing Editor (Production): Cynthia Regan
Senior Production Editor: Anne Graydon
Permissions Coordinator: Charles Morris
Manufacturing Buyer: Michelle Klein
Design and Formatting Manager: Christy Mahon
Cover Design: Kiwi Design
Cover Art Director: Jayne Conte
Cover Photo: Steven Puetzer/Photonica/GettyImages,Inc.
Manager, Multimedia Production: Richard Bretan
Manager, Cover Visual Research & Permissions: Karen Sanatar
Printer/Binder: Command Web

Microsoft® and Windows® are registered trademarks of the Microsoft Corporation in
the U.S.A. and other countries. Screen shots and icons reprinted with permission from
the Microsoft Corporation. This book is not sponsored or endorsed by or affiliated
with the Microsoft Corporation.

Pearson Education LTD.
Pearson Education Singapore, Pte. Ltd
Pearson Education, Canada, Ltd
Pearson Education–Japan

Pearson Education Australia PTY, Limited
Pearson Education North Asia Ltd
Pearson Educación de Mexico, S.A. de C.V.
Pearson Education Malaysia, Pte. Ltd

10 9 8 7 6 5 4 3
ISBN 0-13-221772-4

Dedicated with love to

Art and Sharon
Cippy and Morty
Harry and Deb

Table of Contents

Chapter 1: Introduction

Chapter 2: A Sample Problem

Chapter 3: The Main Menu

Chapter 4: Printing

Chapter 5: Graphs

Chapter 6: Modules

Appendices

Preface

It is hard to believe that *POM-QM for Windows* (formerly *DS for Windows*) has been in existence, first as a DOS program and then as a Windows program, for more than 15 years. It seems as if people have been using both minicomputers and Windows forever but, in fact, large-scale Windows usage has occurred for less than a decade. At the time that I finished the original DOS version, few students had personal computers or knew what an Internet service provider (ISP) was. Today, the large majority of students have their own computers, which makes this software even more valuable than it has ever been.

The original goal in developing this software was to provide students with the most user-friendly package available for production/operations management, quantitative methods, management science, and operations research. We are gratified by the response to the four previous DOS versions and two previous Windows versions of *POM-QM for Windows,* indicating that we have clearly met our goal.

The first version of this software was a DOS version published in 1989 as *PC-POM*. Subsequent DOS versions were titled *AB:POM*. The first Windows version, *QM for Windows* (Version 1.0), was distributed in the summer of 1996 whereas a separate but similar program, *POM for Windows* (Version 1.1), was first distributed in the fall of 1996. *DS for Windows*, which contained all of the modules in both *POM* and *QM* and also came with a printed manual, was first distributed in 1997. Version 2 of all three programs was created for Windows 95 and distributed in the fall of 1999.

For this new version, Version 3, we have collapsed the three former Windows products into one product named *POM-QM for Windows*. For consistency with past versions, when using Prentice Hall texts it is possible to install the program as *POM for Windows* or *QM for Windows* and to display the *POM for Windows* or *QM for Windows* module menu. Regardless of the name of the desktop icon, all of the modules are available to all users. We will refer to the product as *POM-QM for Windows* throughout this manual.

This is a package that can be used to supplement any textbook in the broad area known as Decision Sciences. This includes Production and Operations Management, Quantitative Methods, Management Science, or Operations Research.

Following is a summary of the major changes included in Version 3. These changes fall into three categories: module enhancements, functionality, and user friendliness.

Module Enhancements

In the aggregate planning module, we have added a model to create and solve a transportation model of aggregate planning. For assembly-line balancing, we have added a display that summarizes the minimum number of stations necessary when using each of the available methods. For decision tables, we have added an output display for various values of alpha when computing the Hurwicz value. Our most exciting new addition is that in decision analysis we now have an easy-to-use graphical user interface to create the decision tree. In addition, we have added a new model for creating decision tables for one-period inventory (supply/demand) problems. In forecasting, we have added a model that allows the user to enter the forecasts in order to run an error analysis. In addition, we have added the MAPE as standard output for all models and added forecast control with computation of the tracking signal. In inventory, we have added the reorder point models for both normal and discrete demand distributions. In job shop scheduling, for one-machine sequencing we have allowed for inclusion of the dates that jobs are received and we have added a display that summarizes the results when using all of the methods. In location, we have added a location cost-volume (breakeven) analysis model. In linear programming we display the input in equation form on the right side of the table and have added an output that has the dual model of the original problem. It is also now possible to print the corner points of a graph. In project management, we display the critical path in red. In quality control, it is now possible to set the center line in the control charts rather than using the mean of the data. We have extended our statistics model to include computations for a list of data, a frequency table, or a probability distribution as well as adding a normal distribution model.

Functionality

The formatting and printing options have been improved. It is now possible to format the decimal displays on both the screen and printouts. The right-click options on tables and graphs have been enhanced so that it is now possible to easily copy, print, or save graphs. We have added menu items for inserting multiple columns and multiple rows. When printing, it is possible to select individual graphs to print rather than having to print all of the available graphs. The annotation option has been improved. The Save as Excel option has been expanded to include nearly all of the models. The Windows calculator will be used when found rather than the more primitive calculator that is included with the software. Scroll bars have been added to the forecasting, learning curve and operating characteristic graphs in order to easily display the changes in the graphs as a function of the model parameters.

User Friendliness

As mentioned previously, we have combined all three packages into one package in order that all models will be available to the students – especially students who take both an Operations Management course and a Quantitative Methods course. We still allow for student choice of the menu (POM, QM, or both) to minimize confusion. In addition, in order to improve the understanding of the models we have added separators between models in the model submenu selection menu. We have combined integer and mixed integer programming into one module. We have added an overview tab to the problem creation screen to help describe the options that are available. Manuals (essentially this document) in PDF and Word format have been added so that users may easily access the manual while running the program or print selected pages from the manual. Tutorials that walk you through certain operations step-by-step are included in the Help menu. The examples used in this manual are included in the installation. More user customization options are available in the User Preferences section under the Help menu.

To the students who use this software, I hope you find that this software complements your text well. To the instructors who use this software, thank you for choosing *POM-QM for Windows*. I welcome your comments, especially by e-mail at dsSoftware@prenhall.com.

Acknowledgments

The development of any large scale project such as *POM-QM for Windows* requires the assistance of many people. I have been very fortunate in gaining the support and advice of students and colleagues from around the globe. Without their help, *POM-QM for Windows* would not have been as successful as it has been.

In particular, though I would like to thank the students in Barry Render's classes at Rollins College and the students in my classes at Temple University. These students have always been the first to see the new versions, and over the years several students have offered design features that were incorporated into the software. Other design features were developed in response to comments sent to me from users of the DOS versions and Windows versions 1 and 2. I am extremely grateful for these comments; they have immensely helped the evolution and continuous improvement of *POM-QM for Windows*.

Several changes in the software were put into place in version 3 as a result of the comments of Philip Entwistle, Northampton Business School. The original version of the *POM for Windows* and *QM for Windows* software was reviewed by Dave Pentico of Duquesne University, Laurence J. Moore of Virginia Polytechnic Institute and State University, Raesh G. Soni of Indiana University of Pennsylvania, Donald G. Sluti of the University of Nebraska at Kearney, Nagraj Balachandran of Clemson University, Jack Powell of the University of South Dakota, Sam Roy of Morehead State University, and Lee Volet of Troy State University. Their comments were very influential in the design of the software that has been carried over to the new version.

In addition, other professors who have contributed to this software include Sri Sridharan of Clemson University, Forrest (Fess) Green of Radford University, John E. Nicolay Jr. of the University of Minnesota, Bill Smith of Troy State University, Robert A. Donnel of Goldey-Beacom College, Dave Anstett of the College of St. Scholastica, Leonard Yarbrough of Grand View College, and Cheryl Dale and Steve Moss. Madeline Thinness of Utah State University provided an extensive review of version 2 of the software.

Discussions with Fred Murphy and the late Carl Harris have been very useful to me, especially in the mathematical programming and queueing modules.

There are several individuals at Prentice Hall to whom I must give a special thanks. Rich Wohl and Tom Tucker are the editors with whom I had worked on this project for the first six versions. Not all editors have their keen understanding of computers, software, texts, students, and professors. Without this understanding and vision, *POM-QM for Windows* would still be a vision rather than a reality. My current editors, Alana Bradley and Mark Pfaltzgraf, have been instrumental in getting this version to market. Fellow Prentice Hall authors, including Jay Heizer, Barry Render, Ralph Stair, and Chuck Taylor have helped me to develop the DOS versions and to make the transition from the DOS product to the current Windows products and to improve the Windows product. I am grateful for their many suggestions and the fact that they chose my software as the software to accompany their texts. The support, encouragement, and help from all of these people are very much appreciated. Nancy Welcher provides the support of the Prentice Hall Web pages that are maintained for my products. Finally, I would like to express my appreciation to Debbie Clare who has been the marketing manager for my software.

As always, I must express my appreciation and love to my wife, Lucia, for her understanding and support during the many hours that I have spent and continue to spend in front of my PC improving this software. In addition, I am grateful for the valuable comments and suggestions regarding the look and feel of the software from Lucia and my children, Lisa and Ernie.

Chapter 1

Introduction

Overview

Welcome to Prentice Hall's Decision Science software package: *POM-QM for Windows* (also known as *POM for Windows* and *QM for Windows*). This package is the most user-friendly software package available in the fields of production and operations management, quantitative methods, management science, or operations research. *POM-QM for Windows* has been designed to help you to better learn and understand these fields. The software can be used either to solve problems or to check answers that have been derived by hand. *POM-QM for Windows* contains a large number of models, and most of the homework problems in POM textbooks or QM textbooks can be solved or approached using *POM-QM for Windows*.

In this introduction and the next four chapters, we describe the general features of the software. We encourage you to read them while running the software on your computer. Chapter 6 contains the description of the specific models and applications available in *POM-QM for Windows*.

You will find that the software is extremely user friendly as a result of the following features.

Standardization

The graphical user interface for the software is a standard Windows interface. Anyone familiar with any standard spreadsheet, word processor, or presentation package in Windows easily will be able to use the software. This standard interface includes the customary menu, toolbar, status bar, and help files of Windows programs.

Even though the software contains 29 modules and more than 60 submodels, the screens for every module are consistent, so, after you become accustomed to using one module, you will have an easy time with the other modules.

File storage and retrieval is simple. Files are opened and saved in the usual Windows fashion and, in addition, files are named by module, which makes it easy to find previously saved files.

Data and results, including graphs, can be easily copied and pasted between this application and other Windows applications.

Flexibility

There are several preferences that the user can select from the **Help, User Preferences** menu. For example, the software can be set to automatically save a file after data has been entered or to automatically solve a problem after data has been entered.

The menu of modules can be either a menu that lists only POM models, a menu that lists only QM models, or a menu that list all available models.

The user can select the desired output to print rather than having to print everything. In addition, several print formatting options are available.

The screen components and the colors can be customized by the user. This can be particularly effective for overhead data shows.

User-oriented design

The spreadsheet-type data editor makes data entry and editing extremely easy. In addition, whenever data is to be entered, there is a clear instruction given on the screen describing what is to be entered, and when data is entered incorrectly, a clear error message is displayed.

It is easy to change from one solution method to another in order to compare methods and answers. In several cases, this is simply a one-click operation. In addition, intermediate steps are generally available for display.

The display has been color coded so that answers appear in a different color from data.

Textbook customization

The software can be customized to Prentice Hall textbooks in order that the models, notation, and displays will match the particular textbook.

User support

Updates are available on the Internet through the Prentice Hall Web site for this book, www.prenhall.com/weiss, and help is available by contacting dsSoftware@prenhall.com.

What all of this means to you is that, with a minimal investment of time in learning the basics of *POM-QM for Windows,* you will have an easy-to-use means of solving problems or checking your homework. Rather than being limited to looking at the answers in the back of your textbook, you will be able to see the solutions for most problems. In many cases, the intermediate steps are displayed in order to help you check your work. In addition, you will have the capability to perform sensitivity analysis on these problems or to solve bigger, more interesting problems.

Hardware and Software Requirements

Computer

The software has minimal system requirements. It will run on any IBM PC compatible Pentium machine with at least 8 MB RAM and operating Windows 2000, Windows NT, Windows ME, or Windows XP.

Disk drives/CD-ROM

The software is provided on a CD. This requires a CD-ROM drive for installation.

Monitor

The software has no special monitor requirements. Different colors are used to portray different items, such as data and results. All messages, output, data, and so on will appear on any monitor. Regardless of the type of monitor you use, the software has the capability that allows you to customize colors, fonts, and font sizes in the display to your liking. This is extremely useful when using an overhead projection system. These options are explained in Chapter 3 in the section titled Format.

Printer

A printer is not required to run the software but, of course, if you want a hard copy (printout), then it is necessary to have a printer attached. The printing is standard so that no special features, characters, or printers are required. It also is possible to print to a file in order to import the printout into a word processor for further editing.

Typographic Conventions in this Manual

1. Boldface indicates something that you type or press.

2. Brackets, **[ ]**, name a key on the keyboard or a command button on the screen. For example **[F1]** means Function key F1, whereas **[OK]** means the "Okay" button on the screen.

3.**[Return]**, **[Enter]**, or **[Return/Enter]** indicate the key on your keyboard that has one of those names. The name of the key varies on different keyboards and some even have both keys.

4. Boldface and the capitalized first letter of a term refer to a Windows menu command. For example, **File** refers to the menu command.

5. All capitals refers to a toolbar command, such as SOLVE.

Installing the Software

In the directions that follow, the hard drive is named C: and the CD-ROM is drive D:. The software is installed in the manner that most programs designed for Windows are installed. For all Windows installations, including this one, it is best to be certain that no programs are running while you are installing a new one.

1. Insert the *POM-QM for Windows* CD in drive D:. After a little while, the installation program should begin automatically. If it does not, then:
    a. From the Windows Start Button select, **Run**.
    b. In the box, type **D:setup.pomqmv3.exe** (case does not matter).
    c. Press **[Enter]** or click on **[OK]**.
2. Follow the setup instructions on the screen. Other than the screen that asks for your name, generally speaking, it is simply necessary to click **[NEXT]** each time that the installation asks a question.

Default values have been assigned in the setup program, but you may change them if you would like to do so. The default folder is C:\Program Files\POMQMV3.

The setup program will ask you for registration information, such as your name, university, professor, and course. All items are optional except for the student/user name that must be given. *This name cannot be changed later!* To change the other information from within the program, use **Help, User Information**.

One option that the installation will question you about is whether you want to be able to run the program by double clicking on the file name in File Explorer. If you say "yes", then the program will associate the proper extensions with the program name. This is generally very useful.

Please note that the software installs some files to the Windows system directory. The installation will back up any files that are replaced if you select this option.

If you see a message saying that something is wrong during installation and you have the option of ignoring it, choose this option. The program will likely install properly anyway. The message usually indicates that you are running a program or have run a program that shares a file with this software package. **If you have any installation or operation problems, the first place to check is the download page at www.prenhall.com/weiss.**

Installing and Running on a Network

With the written permission of Prentice Hall, **it is permissible to install the software to a network only if each student has purchased an individual copy of the software.** That is, each student must possess his or her own licensed copy of the CD in order to install the software on a network.

The Program Group

The installation will add a program group with four items to the Start Menu.

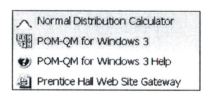

Help is available from within the program, but if you want to read some information about the program without starting it first, use *POM-QM for Windows 3 Help*.

The program group contains one icon named *Prentice Hall Web Site Gateway*. If you have an association for HTML files with a Web browser (e.g., Netscape or Internet Explorer), this document will point you to program updates.

Finally, the software comes with a Normal Distribution Calculator. The calculator is on the Tools menu of the program but also can be used as a stand-alone program without having to open *POM-QM for Windows*.

To uninstall the program use the usual Windows uninstall procedure (**Start, Settings, Control Panel, Add/Remove Programs**). The programs will be removed but the data files will not; they will have to be deleted using My Computer or File Explorer if you wish to do so.

In addition to the Start menu, the installation will place a shortcut to the program on the desktop. The icon appears as the POM-QM icon here:

NOTE: Users who have received this software with their textbook rather than with this manual will see one of the following two icons depending on the textbook.

Starting the Program

The easiest way to start the program is by double-clicking the program icon that is on the desktop. Alternatively, you may use the standard Windows means for starting the program. Click on **Start**, **Programs**, **POM-QM for Windows 3**, **POM-QM for Windows 3** in order to use the software. After starting the program, a splash screen will appear as follows.

Name

The name of the licensee will appear in the display. This should be your name if you are running on a stand-alone computer or the network name if you are running on a network.

Version Number

One important piece of information is the version number of the software. In the example, the version is 3.0 and this manual has been designed around that number. Although this is version 3.0 there is also more detailed information about the program version that can be found using **Help, About** (displayed at the end of Chapter 3). In particular, there is a build number. If you send e-mail asking for technical support, you should include the build number with the e-mail.

NOTE: If the program has been registered as being in a public lab or on a network, then at this point the opening screen will change and give you the opportunity to enter your name. This is useful when you print your results.

The program will start shortly after the opening display appears.

The Main Screen

The second screen that appears is an empty main menu screen.

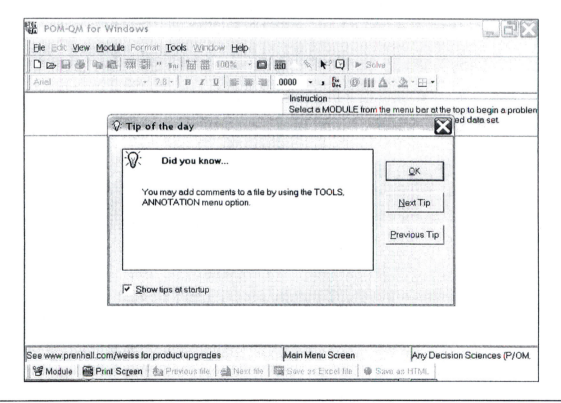

The first time that this screen appears, a Tip of the Day form will appear as displayed above. If you don't want the Tip of the Day to appear each time, then uncheck the box at the lower left of the form. If you change your mind later and want to see the Tip of the Day, go to the **Help** menu.

Please notice the background in the middle of the screen. This is referred to as a gradient. This gradient appears whenever the main screen is empty and it appears on other screens in the software. You may customize the display of the gradient by using **Format, Colors** as explained in Chapter 3.

NOTE: Because this is a printed, black and white manual, the screen colors mentioned will not always appear in the manual. The gradient is the first example of such a situation. For this reason, if you can, you should exam this manual while you are running the program.

After closing the Tip of the Day, or if you have chosen not to see the tips, the next screen is the module selection screen (shown in Chapter 2). In order to display all of the screen components, we have selected a module and loaded a data file.

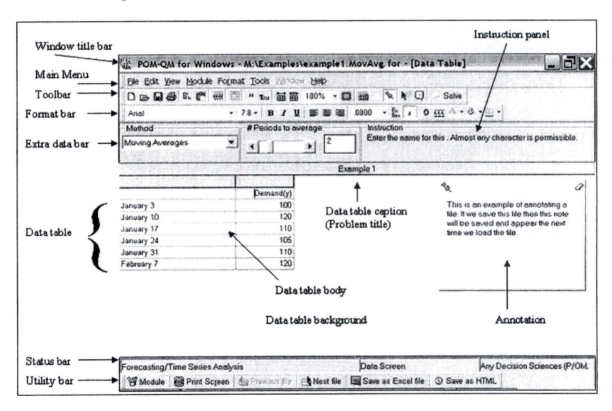

The top of the screen shows the standard Windows title bar for the window. At the beginning the title is *POM-QM for Windows*. If you are using a Prentice Hall text, the names of the authors of the texts should appear in this title bar at the beginning of the program. (If not, go to **Help, User Information**.) The title bar will change to include the name of the file when a file is loaded or saved as shown above. On the left of the title bar is the standard Windows control box and on the right are the standard minimize, maximize, and close buttons for the window-sizing options.

File Edit View Module Format Tools Window Help

Below the title bar is a bar that contains the main menu. The menu bar is very conventional and should be easy to use. The details of the menu options of **File, Edit, View, Module, Format, Tools, Window,** and **Help** are explained in Chapter 3. At the beginning of the program, the **Edit** option is not enabled because there is no data to edit. The **Window** option is also disabled because this refers to results windows and there are as yet no results. Although the menu appears in the standard Windows position at the top of the screen, it can be moved if you like by clicking on the handle on the left and dragging the mouse.

Below the menu is a standard toolbar (also called a button bar or ribbon). This toolbar contains shortcuts for several of the most commonly used menu commands. If you move the mouse over the tool for about 2 seconds, an explanation of the tool (balloon help or tool tip) appears on the screen. As with most software packages, the toolbar can be hidden if you so choose (right click on any of the toolbars or use **View, Toolbars, Customize**). Hiding the toolbar allows for more room on the screen for the problems. As is the case with most toolbars they can float. In order to reposition any of the toolbars, simply click on the handle on the left and drag.

One very important tool on the standard toolbar is the SOLVE ▶ tool on the far right of the toolbar. This is what you press after you have entered the data and you are ready to solve the problem. Alternatively, you may use **File, Solve** or press the **[F9]** key. Please note that after pressing the SOLVE tool, this tool will change to an EDIT ■ tool. This is how you go back and forth from entering data to viewing the solution. For two modules, linear programming and transportation, there is one more command that will appear on the standard toolbar. This is the STEP ✷ tool (not displayed in the figure), and it enables you to step through the iterations, displaying one iteration at a time.

Below the standard toolbar is a format toolbar. This toolbar is very similar to the toolbars found in Excel, Word, and WordPerfect. It too can be customized, moved, hidden, or floated.

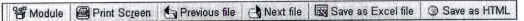

There is one more toolbar, and its default location is at the bottom of the screen. This bar is a utility bar and it contains six tools. The tool on the left is named MODULE. A module list can appear in two ways – either by using this tool or the **Module** option on the main menu. The next tool is named PRINT SCREEN, and it will print the main *POM-QM for Windows* window. The next two tools will load files in alphabetical order either forward or backward. This is very useful when reviewing a number of problems in one chapter, such as the sample files that accompany this manual. The two remaining tools allow files to be saved as Excel or HTML files.

	Demand(y)
January 3	100
January 10	120
January 17	110
January 24	105
January 31	110
February 7	120

Example 1

In the center are two areas, one of which is the main data table. The table contains a heading or title, and rows and columns. The number of rows and columns depends on the module, problem type, and specific problem. The large white area with no grid is the table background. The caption colors, table colors, and background color can be changed by using **Format, Colors,** as explained in Chapter 3.

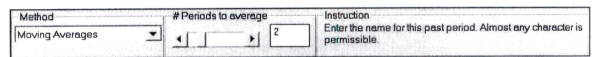

Above the data table is an area named the extra data bar for placing extra problem information. Sometimes it is necessary to indicate whether to minimize or maximize, sometimes it is necessary to select a method, and sometimes some value must be given. These generally appear above the data. On the right of the extra data panel is an instruction panel. There is always an instruction here to help you to determine what to do or what to enter. When data is to be entered into the data table, this instruction will explain what type of data (integer, real, positive, etc.) is to be entered. The instruction location can be changed by using the **View** option.

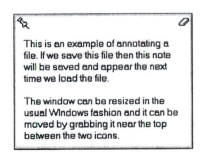

There also is a form for annotating problems. A comment may be placed here. When the file is saved, the information will be saved; when the file is loaded, the information will appear and the annotation may be printed if so desired.

| Forecasting/Time Series Analysis | Data Screen | Any Decision Sciences (P/OM, |

Toward the bottom of the screen is the status bar. The leftmost panel displays the module and submodel name as you select different modules, as exemplified in this illustration where the module is Forecasting and the submodel is Time Series Analysis. The center panel contains the type of screen (data, results, menu, graph, etc.), and the rightmost panel has the textbook name (if a textbook has been selected). The status bar can be hidden by using the **View** option. This panel cannot be moved.

Chapter 2

A Sample Problem

Introduction

In this chapter, a sample problem is examined from beginning to end in order to demonstrate how to use the package. Although not all problems or modules are identical, there is enough similarity among them that seeing one example will make it very easy to use any module in this software. As mentioned in the introduction, the first instruction is to select a module to begin the work.

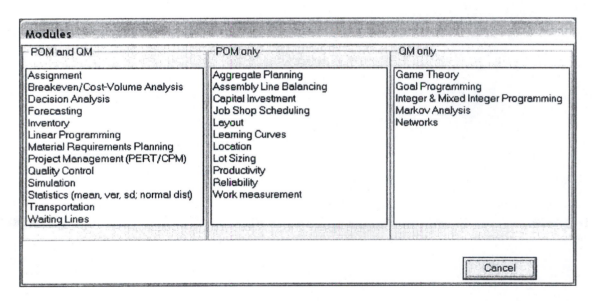

In the preceding figure, the modules are displayed as they are listed when you use the MODULE tool on the utility bar (as opposed to the **Module** option in the main menu at the top). As you can see, there are 29 modules available. They are divided into three groups. The models in the first group typically are included in all POM and QM books, whereas the models in the second group typically appear only in POM books and the models in the third group appear only in QM texts. The models are divided in this fashion so that you will understand it is completely fine to ignore POM-only modules if you have a QM course and vice versa.

If you choose the **Module** option from the main menu, you get the same modules listed in a single list in alphabetical order. (This is displayed in Chapter 3.) You have the option on this menu to display only the POM modules or only the QM modules.

Creating a New Problem

Generally, the first menu option that will be chosen is **File**, followed by either **New**, to create a new data set, or **Open,** to load a previously saved data set. In the figure that follows, we display the creation screen that is used when a new problem is started. Obviously, this is an option that will be chosen very often. The creation screens are similar for all modules, but there are slight differences that you will see from module to module.

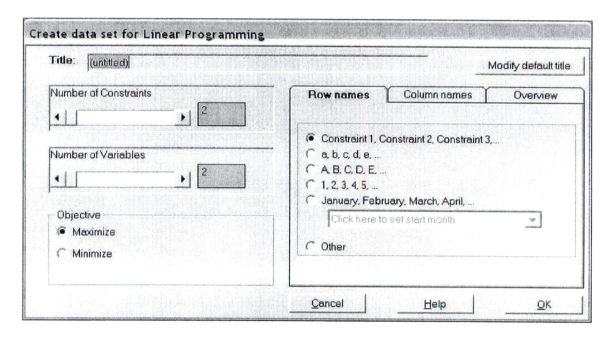

The top line contains a text box into which the title of the problem can be entered. The default title for problems is initially "(untitled)." The default title can be changed by pressing the button [**Modify Default Title**]. For example, if you change the default title to "Homework Problem" then every time you start a new problem the title will appear as Homework Problem, and you would simply need to add the problem number to complete the title. If you want to change the title after creating the problem, this can easily be done by using the **Format, Title** option from the main menu or from the toolbar.

For many modules, it is necessary to enter the number of rows in the problem. Rows will have different names depending on the module. For example, in linear programming, rows are "constraints," whereas in forecasting, rows are "past periods."

At any rate, the number of rows can be chosen with either the scrollbar or the text box. As is usually the case in Windows, they are connected. As you move the scrollbar, the number in the text box changes; as you change the text, the scrollbar moves. In general, the maximum number of rows in any module is 90. There are three ways to add or delete rows or columns after the problem has been created. You may use the options in the **Edit** menu; you may right click on the data table, which will bring up both copy and insert/delete options; or, to insert a single row ▦ or insert a single ▦column, you may use the tools on the toolbar.

This program has the capability to allow you different options for the default row names. Select one of the six option buttons in order to indicate which style of default naming should be used. In most modules, the row names are not used for computations, but you should be careful because in some modules (most notably project management and materials requirements planning) the names might be relevant to the computations. In most modules, the row names can be changed by editing the data table.

Many modules require a number of columns. This is given in the same way as the number of rows. The program gives you a choice of default values for column names in the same fashion as row names but on the Column Names tab.

An overview tab is included on the creation screen in this version of the software. The overview tab gives a brief description of the models that are available and also gives any important information regarding the creation or data entry for that module.

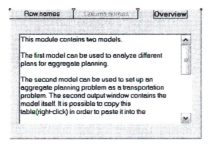

Some modules, such as the linear programming example displayed on the previous page, will have an extra option box, such as for choosing minimize or maximize or selecting whether distances are symmetric. Select one of these options. In most cases, this option can be changed later on the data screen.

When you are satisfied with your choices, click on the **[OK]** button. At this point, a blank data screen will appear, as in the following figure. Screens will differ module by module but they will all resemble the following screen.

The Data Screen

The data screen was described briefly in Chapter 1. It has a data table and, for many models, there is extra information that appears above the data table, such as the objective and starting method as displayed below.

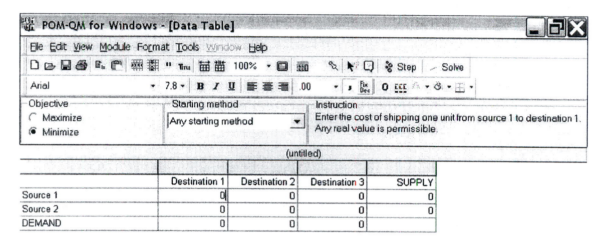

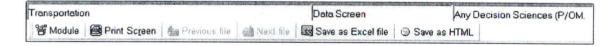

Entering and Editing Data

After a new data set has been created or an existing one has been loaded, the data can be entered or edited. Every entry is in a row and column position. You navigate through the spreadsheet using the cursor movement keys (or the mouse). These keys function in a regular way with one very useful exception – the **[Enter]** key.

The **[Enter]** key takes you to the next cell in the table, first moving to the right and then moving down. When a row is finished, the **[Enter]** key goes to the first cell in the next row that contains data rather than a row name. For example, in the previous screen, if you are at the end of the row named "Source 1" and you press **[Enter]**, the cursor will move to the cell with a "0" in the next row rather than the cell with "Source 2" in it. It is possible to set the cursor to go to the first cell, the one with the name in it, by using **Help, User Information.**

In addition, if you use the **[Enter]** key to enter the data, after you are done with the last cell, the program will automatically solve the problem (saving you the trouble of clicking on the SOLVE tool). This behavior can be adjusted by using **Help, User Information** and, in addition, if you want the program to automatically prompt you to save the file when you are done entering data, this too can be accomplished through **Help, User Information.**

The instruction frame on the screen contains a brief instruction describing what is to be done. There are essentially three types of cells in the data table.

One type is a regular data cell into which you enter either a name or a number. When entering names and numbers, simply type the name or number, then press the **[Enter]** key, one of the direction keys, or click on another cell. If you type an illegal character, a message box will be displayed indicating so.

A second type is a cell that cannot be edited. For example, the empty cell in the upper left-hand corner of the table cannot be edited. (You actually could paste into the cell.)

A third type is a cell that contains a drop-down box. For example, the signs in a linear programming constraint are chosen from this type of box, as shown in the following illustration. To see all of the options, press the arrow on the drop-down box.

	x	y		RHS	Equation form
					Example
Maximize	3	3			Max 3x + 3y
labor hours	3	4	<=	14	3x + 4y <= 14
material (pounds)	6	4	<= ▼	15	6x + 4y <= 15
			<=		
			=		
			>=		

When you are finished entering the data, press the SOLVE tool on the toolbar or use **[F9]** or **File, Solve** and a solution screen will appear as given in the following illustration. The original data is in black and the solution is in a color. Of course, these are only the default values; all colors may be set using **Format, Colors.**

The Solution Screen

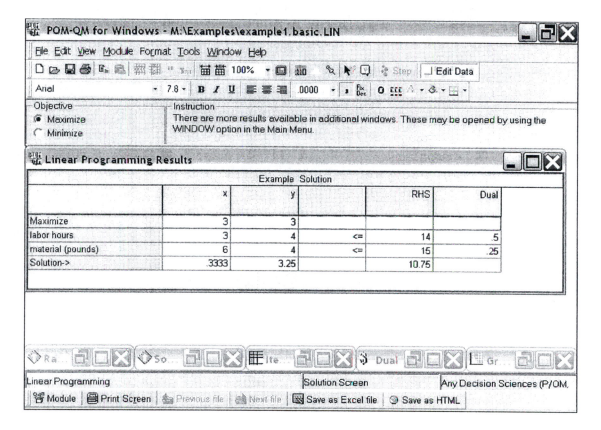

An important thing to notice is that there is more solution information available than the one table displayed. This can be seen by the icons given at the bottom or in the **Window** menu that will automatically drop down. Click on these to view the information.

Alternatively, rather than having the Window menu automatically open when you solve the problem, using **Help, User Information**, you can have the following form open, which gives a little more detail about the solution windows.

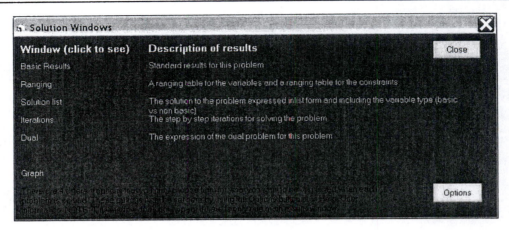

If you click on the OPTIONS button, you can set up the behavior of the software when a problem is solved. The options available here and through **Help, User Information** are as follows:

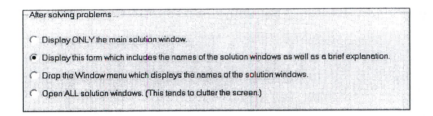

The first option simply displays the solution. The next three options remind you that more results may exist than the one window displayed. The second option displays the Solutions Window, which contains a brief description of each solution Window. The third option automatically drops down the Window menu. These options can be reset using **Help, User Information.**

It is generally at this point that, after reviewing the solution, you would choose to print both the problem and solution.

Now that we have examined the creation and solution of a problem, we explain all of the options that are available in the main menu.

Chapter 3

The Main Menu

File

File contains the usual options that one finds in most Windows programs, as seen in the figure that follows.

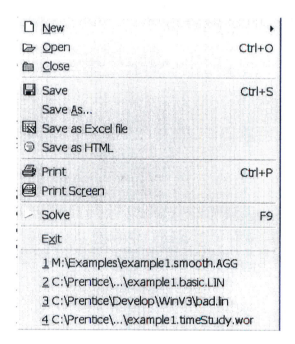

These options are now described.

New ▯

As demonstrated in the sample problem, this option is chosen to begin a new problem (file). In some cases, you will go directly to the problem creation screen, whereas in other cases a pop-up menu will appear indicating the submodels that are available. After selecting a submodel, you will go to the creation screen.

Open 📂

Open is used to open or load a previously saved file. File selection is the standard Windows common dialog type. An example of the screen for opening a file follows. Notice that the extension for files in the software system is given by the first three letters of the module name. For example, all forecasting files have the extension *.for. The exceptions to this rule are assembly-line balancing (*.bal) and layout (*.ope) because of conventions in previous versions and productivity (*.prd) to avoid a conflict with project management. When you go to the Open File dialog, the default value is for the program to look for files of the type in this module. This can be changed at the bottom left, where it says "Files of type." Otherwise, file opening and saving is quite normal. The drive or folder can be changed with the drive/folder drop-down box; a new directory may be created using the new button at the top, and details about the files may be seen by using the details button at the top right.

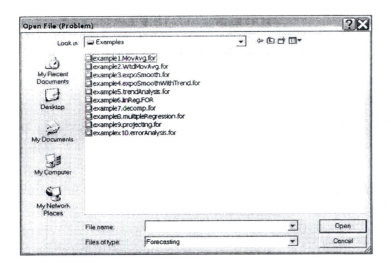

It is possible to use **Help, User Information** to set the program to automatically solve any problem when it gets loaded. This way, if you like, you can be looking at the solution screen whenever you load a problem rather than at the data screen.

Save 💾

Save will replace the file without asking you if you care about overwriting the previous version of this file. If you try to save and have not previously named the file, you will be asked to name this file. That is, the command will function as **Save As**.

Save As

Save As will prompt you for a file name before saving. This option is very similar to the option to load a data file. When you choose this option, the Windows Common Dialog Box for Files will appear. It is essentially identical to the one previously shown for opening files.

The names that are legal are standard Windows file names. In addition to the file name, you may preface the name with a drive letter (with its colon) or path designation. The software will automatically append an extension to the name that you use. As mentioned previously, the extension is the first three letters of the module name. You may type file names in as uppercase, lowercase, or mixed. Examples of legal file names are

sample, sample.tra, c:myFile, c:\myCourse\test, and myproblem.example.

If you enter sample.tra and the module is not transportation, an extension will be added. For example, if the module is linear programming, the name under which the file will be saved will be sample.tra.lin.

Save as Excel File

The software has an option that allows you to save most (but not all) of the problems as Excel files. The data is transported to Excel and the spreadsheet is filled with formulas for the solutions. In some cases, Excel's Solver may be required in order to derive a solution.

For example, following is the output from a waiting line model. The left-hand side has the data, whereas the right-hand side has the solution. Notice the color-coding of the answer vis-a-vis data that appears on the screen but not in this printed manual.

Waiting Lines Results

		Example 1: The M/M/1 queue solution			
Parameter	Value	Parameter	Value	Minutes	Seconds
M/M/1 (exponential service		Average server utilization	.8667		
Arrival rate(lambda)	26	Average number in the queue(Lq)	5.6333		
Service rate(mu)	30	Average number in the system(Ls)	6.5		
Number of servers	1	Average time in the queue(Wq)	.2167	13	780
		Average time in the system(Ws)	.25	15	900

After saving as an Excel file, the Excel file appears below. Notice from the formula for cell E7 (shown at the top of the spreadsheet) that a spreadsheet with formulas was created. That is, we did not "cut and paste" the above screen into Excel (which is possible) but instead created an Excel spreadsheet with appropriate formulas.

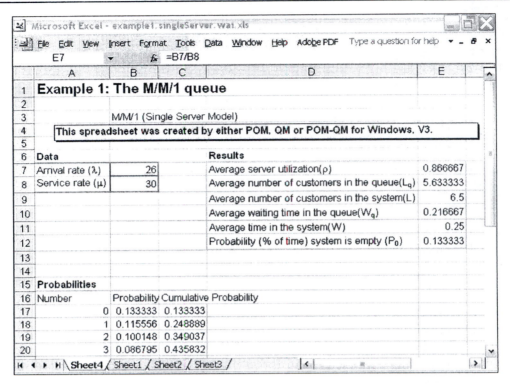

Save as HTML ●

Any table, either data or solution, may be saved as an HTML file, as shown in the following figure.

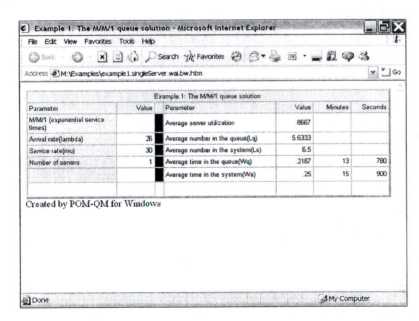

If more than one table is on the screen when this option is selected, the active table is the one that is saved.

Print 🖨

Print will display a Print Setup screen. Printing options are described in Chapter 4. Both **Save** and **Print** act slightly differently if a graph is being displayed at the same time that you use **Print** or **Save**.

Print Screen 🖥

Print Screen will print the screen as it appears. Different screen resolutions may affect the printing. Printing the screen is more time consuming than a regular print. Use this option if you need to demonstrate to your instructor exactly what was on the screen at the time.

Solve ▶

There are several ways to solve a problem. Clicking on **File, Solve** is probably the least efficient way to solve the problem. The toolbar icon may be used, as well as the **[F9]** key. Also, if the data is entered in order (top to bottom, left to right, using **[Enter]**), the program will solve the problem automatically after the last cell.

After solving a problem, the **Solve** ▶ option will change to an **Edit Data** ■ option on both the menu and the toolbar. This is the way to go back and forth between data and solutions. Note that **Help, User Information** may be used to set the program to automatically maximize the solution windows or open all solution windows if so desired.

Step

For the linear programming and transportation modules, a **Step** option will appear both in the **File** menu and on the toolbar.

Exit

The next option on the **File** menu is **Exit**. This will exit the program. You will be asked if you want to exit the program. You can eliminate this question by checking the check box on the form or by using **Help, User Preferences.**

Last Four Files

The **File** menu contains a list of the last four files that you have used. Clicking on one of these will load the file.

Edit

The commands under **Edit** can be seen in the following illustration. Their purposes are threefold. The first six commands are used to insert or delete rows or columns. The second type of command is useful for repeating entries in a column, and the third type is for cutting and pasting between Windows applications. It is also possible to enable the copy options by right clicking on the data or solution table or to enable the insert/delete option by right clicking on the data table.

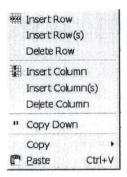

Insert Row ▓ inserts a single row *after* the current row, and **Insert Column** ▓ inserts a single column *after* the current column. **Insert Row(s)** or **Insert Column(s)** asks you how many rows or columns you would like to insert *after* the current row or column. **Delete Row** deletes the current row, and **Delete Column** deletes the current column.

Copy Entry Down Column "

The **Copy Down** command is used to copy an entry from one cell to all cells below it in the column. This is not often useful, but it can save a great deal of work when it is.

Copy

Copy has five options available. It is possible to copy the entire table, the current row, or the current column to the clipboard. It is possible to copy from the data table or any of the solution tables. Whatever is copied can then be pasted into this program or some other Windows program. (The copy tool in the toolbar ▣ copies the entire table.) If you are at the solution stage, the copying will be for the table that is active.

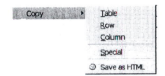

Copy Special copies the entire table but enables you to indicate the number of decimals that are to be copied. **Save as HTML,** which is on this menu for consistency with the right-click menu, performs the HTML operation described previously.

Paste 📋

Paste is used to paste in the current contents of the clipboard. When pasting into *POM-QM for Windows,* the pasting begins at the current cursor position. Thus, it is possible to copy a column to a different column beginning in a different row. This could be done to create a diagonal. It is not possible to paste into a solution table, although, as indicated previously, it is possible to copy from a solution table.

NOTE: Right clicking on any table will bring up **Copy** options, and if the table is the data table, it will also bring up the insert and delete options.

View

View has several options that enable you to customize the appearance of the screen.

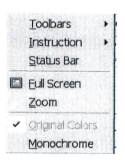

The **Toolbars** menu contains two options. The toolbar can be customized (as can most Windows toolbars) or the toolbar can be reset to its original look.

The **Instruction** bar can be displayed at its default location in the extra data panel, or above the data, below the data, as a floating window, or not at all. The **Status Bar** display can be toggled on or off.

Full Screen 🖵 turns all of the bars (toolbar, command bar, instruction, and status bar) on or off.

Zoom generates a small form allowing you to reduce or increase the size of the columns. It is easier to use the zoom tool `100% ▾` on the standard toolbar. **Zoom** does not zoom in the sense of other programs but instead reduces the column widths. It may be easier to use the squeeze and expand tools on the toolbar than to use **Zoom**.

Colors can be set to **Monochrome** (black and white) or from this state to their **Original Colors**. This formerly was very useful when overhead devices displayed much better in monochrome than in color. Today, projectors are so powerful that monochrome is generally not required.

Module

A drop-down list with all of the modules in alphabetical order will appear. The MODULE tool on the utility toolbar below the data area is a second way to get a list of modules. At the bottom of the list are options for indicating whether you want to display only the POM modules, only the QM modules, or all of the modules as the following display shows.

Aggregate Planning
Assembly Line Balancing
Assignment
Breakeven/Cost-Volume Analysis
Capital Investment
Decision Analysis
Forecasting
Game Theory
Goal Programming
Integer & Mixed Integer Programming
Inventory
Job Shop Scheduling
Layout
Learning Curves
Linear Programming
Location
Lot Sizing
Markov Analysis
Material Requirements Planning
Networks
Productivity
Project Management (PERT/CPM)
Quality Control
Reliability
Simulation
Statistics (mean, var, sd; normal dist)
Transportation
Waiting Lines
Work measurement

Display POM Modules only
Display QM Modules only
✓ Display ALL Modules

Format

Format has several options for the display of data and solution tables, as can be seen in the following illustration. In addition, there are some additional format options available in the format toolbar.

Colors

The colors for all of the displays can be set. There are five tabs, shown as follows. These options create permanent changes, whereas the foreground ⚊ and background ⚊ tools on the format bar change only the current table. Furthermore, the color settings are for the entire table, whereas the format tools may be used for either the entire table or for selected columns.

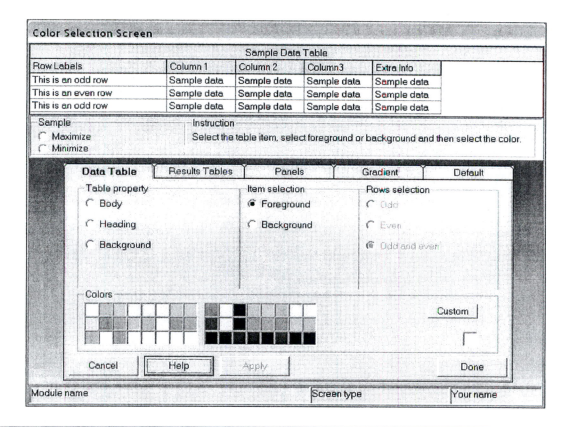

The first tab is for setting the colors in the data table, and the second tab is for setting the colors in the solution tables. That is, it is possible to have the displays of the data and the display of the results appear differently, which can be helpful. For either the data or the results, you may set the background and foreground colors for rows to alternate by using the odd and even options. This makes reading long tables easier.

In order to set the colors, first select the table property that you want to set, then select foreground or background if applicable, then select rows if applicable, and then click on the color. For example, click on **Body, Foreground, Odd,** and then click on the red color box and the foreground for every other row will become red. The changes here will be maintained throughout until you return to this screen and reset the colors. If you want to make changes in only one table for one problem, it may be easier to use the toolbar options for foreground **A** and background. Also, the foreground and background color selection tools, as well as the bold, italic, and underline tools, may be used on individual columns if you select these columns before pressing on the tool.

The third tab allows you to customize the colors in the panels (status, instruction). The fourth tab can be used to set the gradient that appears on several of the screens (problem creation, empty data screen), and the fifth tab allows you to reset the colors to their original (factory) settings.

Other Format Options

The font type, style, and size for all tables can be set. Zeros can be set to display as blanks Ø rather than zeros in the data table. The grid line display can be set to horizontal, vertical, both, or none. The problem title that appears in the data table, and which was created at the creation screen, also can be changed Title .

In order to give some idea of the extensive formatting capabilities available, following is displayed a sample of an overly formatted screen.

Assignment Example							
	Mort	Cippy	*Bruce*	Beth	*Lauren*	Eddie	Brian
Pennsylvania	12	54	34	87	54	89	98
New Jersey	33	45	87	27	34	76	65
New York	12	54	76	23	87	44	62
Florida	15	37	37	65	26	96	23
Canada	42	32	18	77	23	56	87
Mexico	58	71	78	76	82	90	44
Europe	12	34	65	23	44	23	12

In order to create this screen we used **Format, Colors** and changed the background and foreground colors of odd rows to give us the alternating rows. After this we selected the column named "Cippy" and used the background tools on the toolbar to reset the colors for this column only, then we selected "Bruce" and "Lauren" and used the Bold and Italic tools on the toolbar respectively, and, finally, we selected "Brian" and used the foreground tool on the toolbar. (Again, the color display does not show as well in this manual as it does on the screen).

Returning to the **Format** menu, observe that the table can be squeezed ⊞ or expanded ⊞. That is, the column widths can be decreased or increased. Each press of the tool changes the column widths by 10 percent. This is very useful if (results) tables are wider than the screen. The toolbar has the zoom option, which also may be used for resizing the column widths.

NOTE: All tables can have their column widths changed by clicking on the line separating the columns and dragging the column divider left or right. Double clicking on this line will not automatically adjust the column width as it does in Excel.

Number of decimals, **Fixed** and **Comma** are used to format the displayed or printed output. The **Comma** option displays numbers greater than 999 with a comma. The **Number of decimals** drop-down box controls the maximum number of decimals displayed. If you have it set to "00" then .333 would be displayed as .33 whereas 1.5 would be displayed as 1.5. If you turn on the **Fixed** (decimal) option, all numbers would have 2 decimals. Thus, 1.5 would be displayed as 1.50 and line up with 1.33.

The input can be checked or not. It is a good idea to always check the input, but not checking allows you to put entries into cells that otherwise could not be put there.

The last option of **Insert/Delete** takes you to the Edit menu.

Tools

The software should find the Windows calculator if you select the **Calculator** ▦ option. If not, a calculator is available for simple calculations, including square roots. Numbers may be copied from the calculator and pasted into an individual cell in the data table. A **Normal Distribution Calculator** ▲ is available for performing calculations related to the normal distribution. This is particularly useful for forecasting and project management. See the **Help** screen for information on how to use the Normal Distribution Calculator, or use the happy face on the calculator to get step-by-step instructions. An example of the Normal Calculator appears in Chapter

6 in the section on project management. The same computations can be done in the statistics module but the calculator is a little more intuitive to use.

There is an area available to **Annotate** ✎ problems. If you want to write a note to yourself about the problem, select **Annotate**. The note will be saved with the file if you save the file. An example of annotation appears in Chapter 1. In order to eliminate the annotation completely, the box must be blank (by deleting) and then the file must be resaved. When you print, you have an option to print the note or not.

Window

A sample of the Window options appears in the next illustration. This menu option is enabled only at the solution screen. Notice that in this example there are six different output screens that can be viewed. The number of windows depends on the specific module and problem.

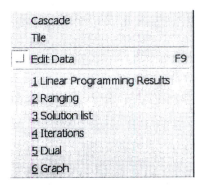

Following is a display of the screen after using the **Tile** option from the **Window** menu when the screen resolution was set to 1280 by 1024. With this resolution it may be very useful to tile in order to see all of the available solution windows. In fact, using **Help, User Information,** you could set all solution windows to open up for every problem. Obviously, the value of this option depends on your screen resolution.

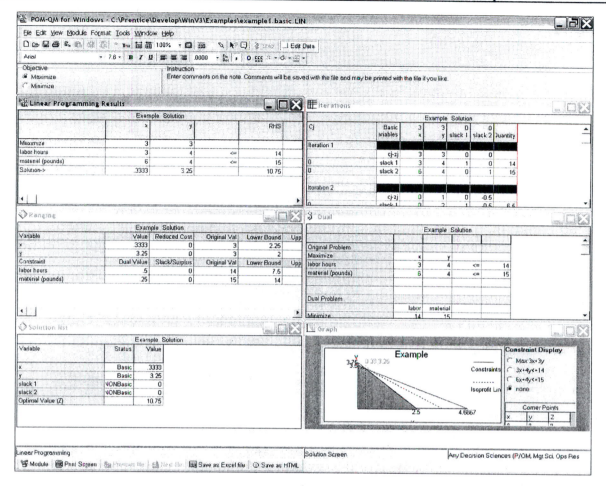

Help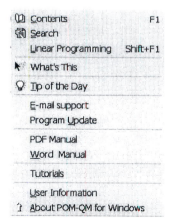

The **Help** options are displayed next.

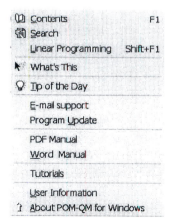

The third option is the topic; it gives a description of the module, the data required for input, the output results, and the options available in the module. It is worthwhile to look at this screen at least one time in order to be certain that there are no unsuspected differences between your assumptions and the assumptions of the program. If there is anything to be warned about regarding the option, it will appear on the help screen as well as in Chapter 6 of this manual.

Tip of the Day ☀

The **Tip of the Day** will be displayed. From this option, it is possible to set the tip to display all of the time or not to display.

E-mail support

E-mail support uses your e-mail to set up a message to be sent to Prentice Hall. The first step is to click on the main body of the message and then to paste (CTRL-V or SHIFT-INS) the information that the program has created into the body of the e-mail.

Program Update

Program Update points you to www.prenhall.com/weiss Updates are on the download page.

Manuals

The program comes with this manual in both PDF form and as a Word document. The PDF manual requires Adobe acrobat reader, which is available free through http://www.adobe.com/.

Tutorials

The program comes with tutorials that are Macromedia Flash displays (exe files), which show you how to perform certain operations.

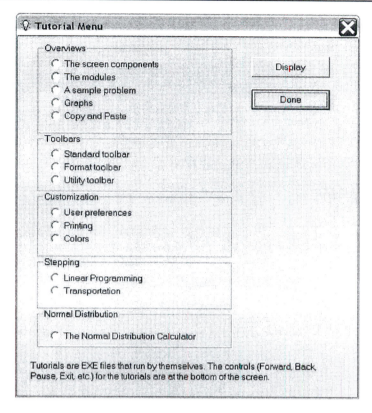

User Information

The user information form is shown as follows. The first tab can be used to change the name of the course, instructor, or school. The student name is set at the time of installation of the software and cannot be changed.

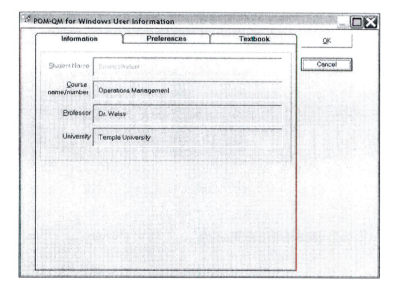

The second tab is used to set several of the options that have been discussed to this point.

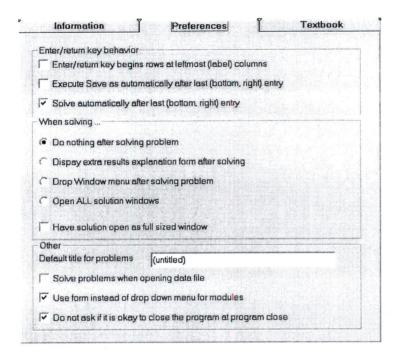

The third tab is used to set the textbook. There are differences among displays, models available, and computations for different textbooks. The list of textbooks will change over time as new textbooks are added.

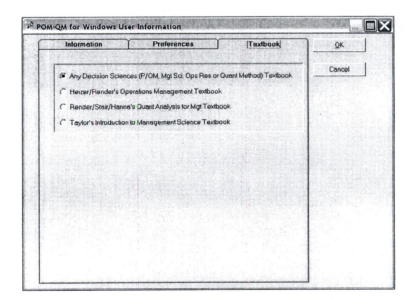

About POM-QM for Windows

The last help option is a standard About display. Notice the build number (Build 20) after the version number. If you send e-mail requesting help, please be sure to include this build number. Also, notice the Web site location – www.prenhall.com/weiss. This site contains updates!

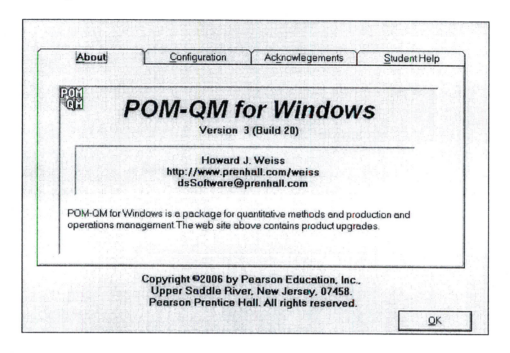

Chapter 4

Printing

The Print Setup Screen

After selecting **Print** 🖨 from the menu (or toolbar), the Print Setup screen will be displayed as shown in the accompanying figure. There are several options on this screen that are divided over five tabs. The first tab is shown in the figure.

Before examining the tabs, please notice that the bottom of the form contains three frames that, if clicked, will change the format among black/white and color, portrait and landscape, and ASCII and grid-style printing. The same options appear on the tabs but access to the options is more direct here.

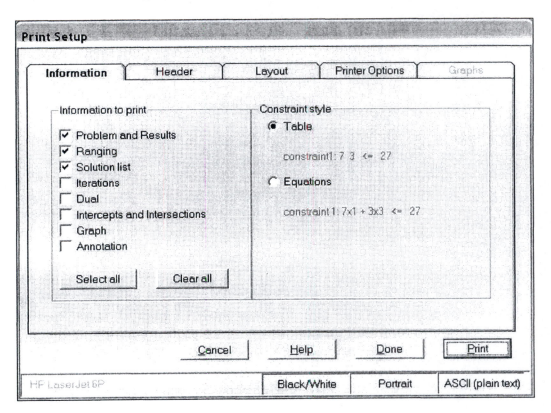

Information to Print

The options in the frame depend on whether **Print** was selected from the data screen or from the solution screen. From the data screen, the only option that will appear is to print the data. However, from the solution screen, there will be one option for each screen of solution values.

For example, in the preceding linear programming example there are six different output displays as well as an available graph and annotation because this file had a note attached. You can select which of these will be printed. In general, the data is printed when printing the output, and, therefore, it is seldom necessary to print the data, meaning that all printing can be performed after the problem is solved.

Tables versus Equations

For mathematical programming types of modules, there is an option available about the style of printing. The problem can be printed in regular tabular form or in equation form. Examples of each follow.

Tabular Form

```
Results ----------
                  X      Y                    RHS      Dual
Maximize          3      3
labor hours       3      4        <=          14       0.5
material (pounds) 6      4        <=          15       0.25
```

Equation Form

```
Results ----------
OPTIMIZE: 3x + 3y
labor hours:+ 3x + 4y <= 14
material (pounds):+ 6x + 4y <= 15
```

Printing Graphs

If multiple graphs are available, the software will allow you to select which graphs should be printed. For example, project management results include three Gantt charts and a precedence graph. You can select which graphs you would like from the list that is presented as shown in the following figure.

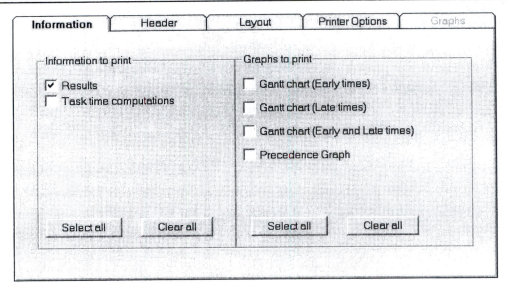

If all you want is one of the graphs, it is also possible to do your graph printing from the graph screen (described in the next chapter) rather than from the results screen. Furthermore, if you want to control the size of the printed graph, use the options presented in the next chapter.

Page Header Information

The tab for the page header information is displayed as follows. There are six pieces of information that can be chosen to appear on the header. The first three options will appear on the first header line, and the second three will appear on the second header line. To make permanent changes to the course name or instructor name, use **Help, User Information.**

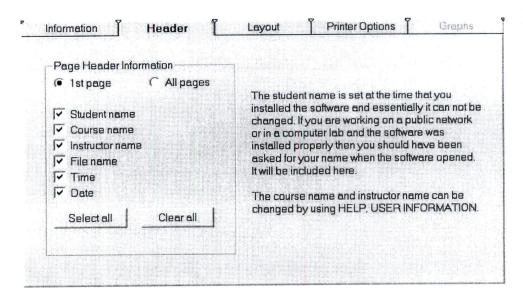

Page Layout

The tab for page layout displays as follows.

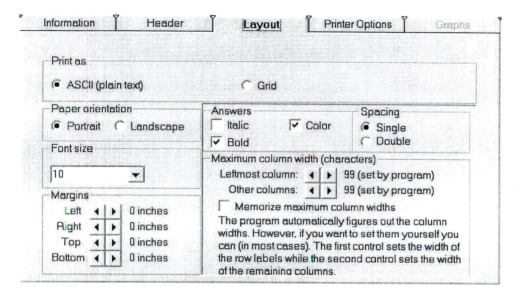

Print As

There are two styles of printing that may be used. The most common and fastest way to print is as ASCII (plain text). In addition, you may also print a grid, similar to the one that appears on the screen. Thus, you may format the grid, then go to the print option, and print a highly formatted grid. The formatted grids take longer to print than the plain text.

Paper Orientation

The paper can be printed in regular fashion (portrait) or it can be printed sideways (landscape) if you need more space for columns.

Answers

Answers can be bold, italic, color, or any combination of the three. Do not opt for color if you do not have a color printer. In fact, if you set the printing to use color on a black/white printer, the color answers generally appear lighter! This usually is not the desired characteristic. The program should properly identify whether the printer is color at the time of installation.

Spacing

The printing may be single-spaced (highly suggested) or double-spaced.

Margins

The left, right, top, and bottom margins can be set from 0 to 1 inch in increments of .1 inches. The margin is above or beyond any natural margin that the printer itself has. Margins of 0 allow for the most printing across the page.

Maximum Column Widths

The maximum widths of the columns (in characters) can be set. The leftmost column, which usually consists of names, can be set separately from the other columns. This is useful if you want to compress tables.

Printer Options

The tab for the printer options appears as follows.

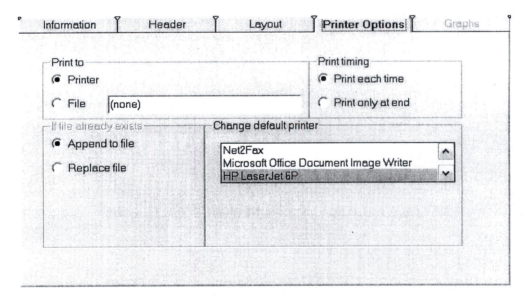

Print to and If File Already Exists

It is possible to print to the printer or to print to a file. If you print to a file, you will be asked for a file name. Any name can be given. You also have the option of adding the printing to a file that was already there (appending) or erasing the file before printing (replace file). It is not possible to print graphs to a file.

If you have Microsoft Office 2003, you can also use the Microsoft Office Document Image Writer "printer" to print to a file. Microsoft Document Images cannot be edited but graphs can be printed to these files.

Print Timing

Printing can occur each time that you use Print or at the end, when everything will be printed at once. Printing each time is generally preferable, but there are some situations where you want to wait until the end because this may save paper or minimize the number of trips to a network printer.

Change Default Printer

If you have more than one printer, you may change the printer using this option. This changes the Windows default printer and may affect other programs! If you print as a grid, the printer selected is always the Windows default printer regardless of what you select in this window.

Chapter 5

Graphs

Introduction

Many of the modules have the capability to display graphs or charts as one of the output options. Some of the modules have more than one graph associated with them. For example, as shown in the following figure, four different project management graphs are available. The graph to be displayed is chosen using the tab. There are several options that you have when a graph appears, and those options are explained in this chapter.

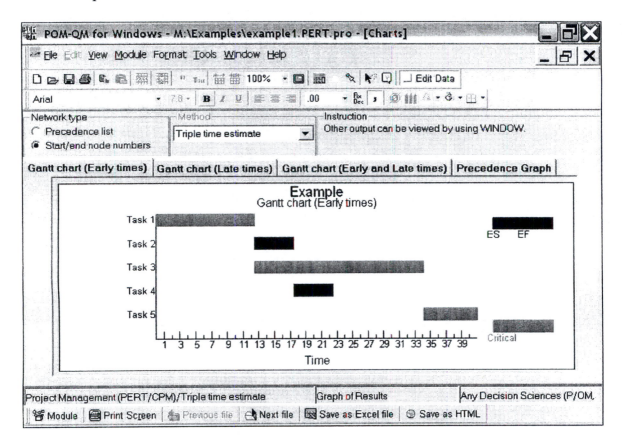

When a graph is opened, two things occur. First, the graph will be displayed covering the entire area below the extra data; and second, some of the menu options will change or execute differently.

File Saving

The file save option 💾 both under **File** on the main menu and on the toolbar will save the (active) graph rather than saving the file. The file may still be saved by using **File, Save as** or by going to a results window other than the graph window.

Printing

Print 🖨 now will print the graph rather than presenting the general print setup screen. The print graph options are shown in the following figure. The graph can be printed in two sizes, and can be printed as either portrait (8.5 by 11) or landscape (11 by 8.5). Small graphs can be printed at the top or bottom of the page. Thus, there is slightly more customization of graph printing available through this method than when printing the graphs as part of the output, as described in the previous chapter.

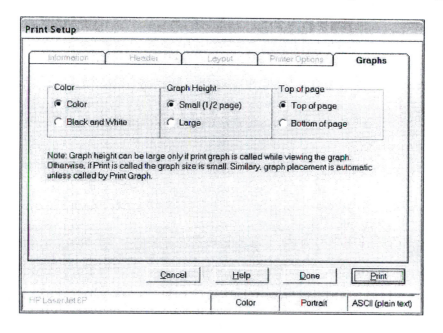

Colors and Fonts

The foreground ⏷ colors and the background 🎨 colors may be changed by using the tools on the format toolbar. Changing the font name on the toolbar will change the font for the headings and labels in the graphs. Clicking on bold on the toolbar will change the font in the graphs to bold.

Chapter 6

Modules

Overview

In this chapter, each of the 29 modules is detailed. The input required for each module, the options available for modeling and solving, and the different output screens and reports that can be seen and printed are explained. Recall that the menu can be set to display only POM modules, only QM modules or all modules. In this manual, for modules that are in both the POM and QM menus we display the *POM-QM for Windows* icon:

 .

For all modules that are in the POM-only menu, we display the *POM for Windows* icon:

For all modules that are in the QM-only menu, we display the *QM for Windows* icon,

For example, in the first module, aggregate planning, which begins on the next page, the POM icon is presented because aggregate planning is typically a topic in Operations Management courses but not in Management Science courses and thus appears in the *POM-only menu* but not in the *QM-only menu*. Finally, the examples used in this manual have been installed in the Examples folder in the POM-QM for Windows folder (Program Files\POMQMV3).

Aggregate (Production) Planning

Production planning is the means by which production quantities for the medium term (generally one year) are determined. Aggregate planning refers to the fact that the production planning is usually carried out across product lines. We will use the terms aggregate planning and production planning interchangeably. The main planning difficulty is that demands vary from month to month. Production should remain as stable as possible yet it should maintain minimum inventory and experience minimum shortages. The costs of production, overtime, subcontracting, inventory, shortages, and changes in production levels must be balanced.

In some cases, aggregate planning problems might require the use of the transportation or linear programming modules. The second submodel in the aggregate planning module creates and solves a transportation model of aggregate planning for cases where all of the costs are identical. The transportation model is also available as one of the methods in the list of models for the first submodel.

The Aggregate Planning Model

Production planning problems are characterized by a demand schedule, a set of capacities, various costs, and a method for handling shortages. Consider the following example.

Example 1: Smooth production

Consider a situation where demands in the next four periods are for 1200, 1500, 1900, and 1400 units. Current inventory is 0 units. Suppose that regular time capacity is 2000 units per month and that overtime and subcontracting are not considerations. The costs are $8 for each unit produced during regular time, $3 for each unit held per period, $4 for each unit short per period, $5 for each unit by which production increases from the previous period, and $6 for each unit by which production is reduced from the previous period. The screen for this example is displayed below.

In addition to the data, we have two considerations – shortage handling and the method to use for performing the planning. These are handled in the extra data bar above the data table.

Shortage handling. In production planning there are two models for handling shortages. In one model, shortages are backordered. That is, demands can accumulate and be met in later periods. In another model, the shortages become lost sales. That is, if you cannot satisfy the demand in the period in which it is requested, the demand disappears. This option is above the data table.

Shortages	Method	Instruction
⊙ Backordered ○ Lost sales	Smooth production (Average GROSS c ▼	Enter the name for this period. Almost any character is permissible.

Period	Demand	Regular time Capacity	Overtime Capacity	Subcontract Capacity		Unit costs	Value
Pd1	1,200	2,000	0	0		Regular time	8
Pd2	1,500	2,000	0	0		Overtime	9
Pd3	1,900	2,000	0	0		Subcontracting	11
Pd4	1,400	2,000	0	0		Holding cost	3
						Shortage cost	4
						Increase cost	5
						Decrease cost	6
						Initial Inventory	0
						Units last period	0

Methods.

Six methods are available, which will be demonstrated. Please note that smooth production accounts for two methods.

Smooth production will have equal production in every period. This yields two methods because the production quantities can be determined according to the gross demand or the net demand (gross demand minus initial inventory).

Produce to demand will create a production schedule that is identical to the demand schedule.

Constant regular time production, followed by overtime and subcontracting if necessary. The lesser cost method will be selected first.

Any production schedule: in which case the user must enter the amounts to be produced in each period.

The transportation model. This method yields the same transportation model as the second submodel from the **File, New** menu.

Quantities

Demand. The demands are the driving force of aggregate planning and these are given in the first column of data.

Capacities – regular time, overtime, and subcontracting. The program allows for three types of production – regular time, overtime, and subcontracting, – and capacities for these are to be given in the next three columns. If the method selected is the user-defined method, these columns are not viewed as capacities but rather as production quantities. When deciding whether to use overtime or subcontracting, the program will always first select the one that is less expensive.

Costs

The costs for the problem are all placed in the far right column of the data screen.

Production costs – regular time, overtime, and subcontracting. These are the per-unit production costs depending on when and how the unit is made.

Inventory (holding) cost. This is the amount charged for holding 1 unit for 1 period. The total holding cost is charged against the ending inventory. Be careful; although most textbooks charge against the ending inventory, some textbooks charge against average inventory during the period.

Shortage cost. This is the amount charged for each unit that is short in a given period. Whether it is assumed that the shortages are backlogged and satisfied as soon as stock becomes available in a future month or are lost sales is indicated by the option box above the data table. Shortage costs are charged against end-of-month levels.

Cost to increase production. This is the cost that results from having changes in the production schedule. It is given on a per-unit basis. The cost for increasing production entails hiring costs. It is charged against the changes in the amount of regular time production but not charged against any overtime or subcontracting production volume changes. If the initial production level is zero, there will be no charge for increasing production in the first period.

Cost to decrease production. This is similar to the cost of increasing production and is also given on a per-unit basis. However, this is the cost for reducing production. It is charged only against regular time production volume changes.

Other Considerations

Initial inventory. Oftentimes we have a starting inventory from the end of the previous month. The starting inventory is placed in the far right column toward the bottom.

Units last period. Because some of the costs are for changes in production quantities from period to period, it is necessary to include the production in the period prior to the start of the problem. These units appear in the far right column at the bottom.

The Solution

In the first example, shown in the following screen, the smooth production method and backorders have been chosen. The demands are 1200, 1500, 1900, and 1400, and the regular time capacity of 2000 exceeds this demand. There is no initial inventory. The numbers represent the production amounts. The costs can be seen toward the bottom of the columns. The screen contains information on both a period-by-period basis and on a summary basis. Notice the color coding of the data (black), intermediate computations (magenta), and results (blue).

Aggregate Planning Results					
Example 1 - Smooth production solution					
	Demand	Regular time Capacity	Regular time production	Inventory (end PD)	Shortage (end PD)
Initial Inventory				0	
Pd1	1,200	2,000	1,500	300	0
Pd2	1,500	2,000	1,500	300	0
Pd3	1,900	2,000	1,500	0	100
Pd4	1,400	2,000	1,500	0	0
Total(units)	6,000	8,000	6,000	600	100
			@$8 /unit	@$3 /unit	@$4 /unit
Subtotal Costs			$48,000	$1,800	$400
Total Cost	$50,200				

Regular time production. The amount to be produced in regular time is listed in the "Regular time production" column. This amount is determined by the program for all options except User Defined. In this example, because the gross (or net) demand is 6000, there are 1500 units produced in regular time in each of the 4 periods. If the total demand is not an even multiple of the number of periods, extra units will be produced in as many periods as necessary in order to meet the demand. For example, had the total demand been 6002, the production schedule would have been 1501 in the first and second periods and 1500 in the other two periods.

The ending inventory is represented by one of two columns – either "Inventory" or "Shortage."

Inventory (holding). The accumulated inventory appears in this column if it is positive. In the example, there is a positive inventory of 300 units in Periods 1 and 2, no inventory (actually a shortage) in Period 3, and neither any inventory nor shortage at the end of Period 4.

Shortages. If there is a shortage, the amount of the shortage appears in this column. In the example, the 100 in the shortage column for period 3 means that 100 units of demand have not been met. Because the backlog option has been chosen, the demands are met as soon as possible, which is in the last period.

No increase or decrease from month to month occurs, so these columns do not appear in this display.

Total. The total number of units demanded, produced, in inventory, short, or in increased and decreased production are computed. In the example, 6000 units were demanded, 6000 units were produced, and there was a total of 600 unit-months of inventory, 100 unit-months of shortage, and 0 increased or decreased production unit-months.

Costs. The totals of the columns are multiplied by the appropriate costs, yielding the total cost for each of the cost components. For example, the 600 units in inventory have been multiplied by $3 per unit, yielding a total inventory cost of $1800, as displayed.

Total cost. The overall total cost is computed and displayed. For this strategy, the total cost is $50,200.

Graph

Two graphs are available in this module.

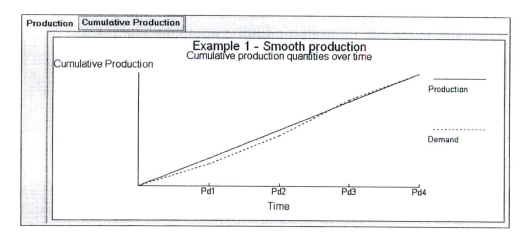

It is possible to display a bar graph of production in each period (not shown), and it is also possible to display a graph of the cumulative production versus the cumulative demand (shown above).

Example 2: Starting inventory and previous production

Two modifications to the previous example have been made. These modifications can be seen in the following screen. In the "Initial Inventory" location, 100 is used. In addition, the method to use has been changed to use the net demand.

Shortages	Method	Instruction
⦿ Backordered	Smooth production (Average NET dem ▼)	Enter the name for this period. Almost any character is permissible.
○ Lost sales		

Example 2 - Smooth production (net demand) and initial inventory

Period	Demand	Regular time Capacity	Overtime Capacity	Subcontract Capacity		Unit costs	Value
Pd1	1,200	2,000	0	0		Regular time	8
Pd2	1,500	2,000	0	0		Overtime	9
Pd3	1,900	2,000	0	0		Subcontracting	11
Pd4	1,400	2,000	0	0		Holding cost	3
						Shortage cost	4
						Increase cost	5
						Decrease cost	6
						Initial Inventory	100
						Units last period	0

Examining the "Regular time production" column in the output that follows indicates that the total production is 5900 rather than the 6000 from the previous example as a result of the initial inventory. Thus, only 1475 units per month need to be produced.

Aggregate Planning Results

Example 2 - Smooth production (net demand) and initial inventory solution

	Demand	Regular time Capacity	Regular time production	Inventory (end PD)	Shortage (end PD)
Initial Inventory				100	
Pd1	1,200	2,000	1,475	375	0
Pd2	1,500	2,000	1,475	350	0
Pd3	1,900	2,000	1,475	0	75
Pd4	1,400	2,000	1,475	0	0
Total(units)	6,000	8,000	5,900	725	75
			@$8 /unit	@$3 /unit	@$4 /unit
Subtotal Costs			$47,200	$2,175	$300
Total Cost	$49,675				

Example 3: Using overtime and subcontracting

In the next example shown in the following screen, the original example (without starting inventory) is used but the capacity for regular time is reduced to 1000 units per period. We have included capacities of 100 for overtime and 900 for subcontracting, as well as unit costs for overtime and subcontracting of $9 and $11, respectively. This can be seen as follows.

Shortages	Method	Instruction
⦿ Backordered ○ Lost sales	Smooth production (Average NET dem ▼)	There are more results available in additional windows. These may be opened by using the WINDOW option in the Main

Aggregate Planning Results _ □ ✕

Example 3 - Overtime and subcontracting solution

	Demand	Regular time Capacity	Overtime Capacity	Subcontract Capacity	Regular time production	Overtime production	Subcontracting	Inventory (end PD)	Shortage (end PD)
Initial Inventory								0	
Pd1	1,200	1,000	100	900	1,000	100	400	300	0
Pd2	1,500	1,000	100	900	1,000	100	400	300	0
Pd3	1,900	1,000	100	900	1,000	100	400	0	100
Pd4	1,400	1,000	100	900	1,000	100	400	0	0
Total(units)	6,000	4,000	400	3,600	4,000	400	1,600	600	100
					@$8 /unit	@$9 /unit	@$11 /unit	@$3 /unit	@$4 /unit
Subtotal Costs					$32,000	$3,600	$17,600	$1,800	$400
Total Cost	$55,400								

Because there is not enough regular time capacity, the program looks to overtime and subcontracting. It first chooses the one that is less expensive. Therefore, in this example, the program first makes 1000 units on regular time, then 100 units on overtime ($9/unit), then 400 units (of the 900 available) on subcontracting ($11/unit).

Example 4: When subcontracting is less expensive than overtime

The following screen, shows a case where subcontracting is less expensive than overtime. That is, the only change made from the previous screen is to make the overtime cost $13 rather than $9. This time, the program first chooses subcontracting and, since there is sufficient capacity, overtime is not used at all.

Shortages
● Backordered
○ Lost sales

Method
Smooth production (Average NET dem ▼)

Instruction
There are more results available in additional windows. These may be opened by using the WINDOW option in the Main

Aggregate Planning Results   ▬ ◻ ✕

Example 4 - Overtime more expensive than subcontracting solution

	Demand	Regular time Capacity	Overtime Capacity	Subcontract Capacity	Regular time production	Subcontracting	Inventory (end PD)	Shortage (end PD)
Initial Inventory							0	
Pd1	1,200	1,000	100	900	1,000	500	300	0
Pd2	1,500	1,000	100	900	1,000	500	300	0
Pd3	1,900	1,000	100	900	1,000	500	0	100
Pd4	1,400	1,000	100	900	1,000	500	0	0
Total(units)	6,000	4,000	400	3,600	4,000	2,000	600	100
					@$8 /unit	@$11 /unit	@$3 /unit	@$4 /unit
Subtotal Costs					$32,000	$22,000	$1,800	$400
Total Cost	$56,200							

Example 5: Lost sales – case 1

From the previous example lost sales are used rather than backorders, as can be seen in the following screen.

Shortages
○ Backordered
● Lost sales

Method
Smooth production (Average NET dem ▼)

Instruction
There are more results available in additional windows. These may be opened by using the WINDOW option in the Main

Aggregate Planning Results   ▬ ◻ ✕

Example 5 - Lost sales solution

	Demand	Regular time Capacity	Overtime Capacity	Subcontract Capacity	Regular time production	Subcontracting	Inventory (end PD)	Shortage (end PD)
Initial Inventory							0	
Pd1	1,200	1,000	100	900	1,000	500	300	0
Pd2	1,500	1,000	100	900	1,000	500	300	0
Pd3	1,900	1,000	100	900	1,000	500	0	100
Pd4	1,400	1,000	100	900	1,000	500	100	0
Total(units)	6,000	4,000	400	3,600	4,000	2,000	700	100
					@$8 /unit	@$11 /unit	@$3 /unit	@$4 /unit
Subtotal Costs					$32,000	$22,000	$2,100	$400
Total Cost	$56,500							

The output shows a shortage of 100 units at the end of period 3. In the next period, we produce 1500 units even though we need only 1400 units. These extra 100 units are not used to satisfy the Period 3 shortage, because these have become lost sales. The 100 units go into inventory, as can be seen from the inventory column in Period 4. It does not make sense to use the smooth production model and have lost sales. In the end, the total demand is not really 6000, because 100 of the sales were lost.

Example 6: The produce-to-demand (no inventory) strategy

From the first example, the method has been changed to a produce to demand or chase strategy as can be seen in the following screen.

	Demand	Regular time Capacity	Regular time production	Units increase	Units decrease
Initial Inventory					
Pd1	1,200	2,000	1,200	0	0
Pd2	1,500	2,000	1,500	300	0
Pd3	1,900	2,000	1,900	400	0
Pd4	1,400	2,000	1,400	0	500
Total(units)	6,000	8,000	6,000	700	500
			@$8 /unit	@$5 /unit	@$6 /unit
Subtotal Costs			$48,000	$3,500	$3,000
Total Cost	$54,500				

Shortages: ● Backordered ○ Lost sales

Method: Chase CURRENT demand (let workfor ▼)

Instruction: There are more results available in additional windows. These may be opened by using the WINDOW option in the Main

Aggregate Planning Results

Example 6 - Produce to Demand Solution

Notice that the program has set the "Regular time production" column equal to the demand column. The inventory is not displayed because it is always 0 under this option. With production equal to demand, and no starting inventory, there will be neither changes in inventory nor any shortages. The production rates will increase or decrease. In this example, production in Period 1 was 1200 and production in Period 2 was 1500. Therefore, the increase column has a 300 in it for Period 2. The program will not list any increase in Period 1 if no initial production is given. The total increases have been 700; decreases 500.

Increase. The change in production from the previous period to this period occurs in this column if the change represents an increase. Notice that the program assumes that no change takes place in the first period in this example. In this example, there is no change in other periods because production is constant under the smooth production option.

Decrease. If production decreases, the decrease appears in this column.

Example 7: Increase and decrease charging

The previous example had increases and decreases in production. These increases and decreases are accounted for by regular time production. In the following screen, the regular time capacity is reduced in order to force production through regular time and overtime.

Shortages
- ⦿ Backordered
- ○ Lost sales

Method
Chase CURRENT demand (let workfor ▼)

Instruction
There are more results available in additional windows. These may be opened by using the WINDOW option in the Main

Aggregate Planning Results ▯□✕

Example 7 - Chase demand solution

	Demand	Regular time Capacity	Overtime Capacity	Subcontract Capacity	Regular time production	Overtime production	Units increase	Units decrease
Initial Inventory								
Pd1	1,200	1,500	500	500	1,200	0	0	0
Pd2	1,500	1,500	500	500	1,500	0	300	0
Pd3	1,900	1,500	500	500	1,500	400	0	0
Pd4	1,400	1,500	500	500	1,400	0	0	100
Total(units)	6,000	6,000	2,000	2,000	5,600	400	300	100
					@$8 /unit	@$9 /unit	@$5 /unit	@$6 /unit
Subtotal Costs					$44,800	$3,600	$1,500	$600
Total Cost	$50,500							

Notice that the increase column only has a value in it in the second period when regular time production went from 1200 to 1500 units. The regular time production remains at 1500; even though overtime increases, this does not show up in the increase columns. There are no charge against such increases.

Example 8: The transportation model of aggregate planning

The transportation model of aggregate planning contains data that is nearly identical to the models previously examined. The only difference is that the transportation model does not consider changes in production levels, so there is no data entry allowed for increase and decrease costs or for units last period. The creation screen will ask for the number of periods and whether shortages are allowed or not. The similarity to the previous screens can be seen in the screen that follows. Notice that there is only one entry for each of the costs. Thus, this model cannot be used for situations where the costs change from period to period. You must formulate these problems yourself using the transportation model from the module menu rather than this transportation submodel of aggregate planning.

NOTE: The transportation model that is the second submodel in the **New** menu can also be accessed as the last method in the first submodel.

Shortages	Instruction
⦿ Not allowed	Enter the name for this period. Almost any character is permissible.
○ Backordered	

Example 8: Aggregate planning as a transportation model

Period	Demand	Regular tm Capacity	Overtime Capacity	Subcontract Capacity		Unit costs	Value
Spring	800	800	100	750		Regular time	27
Summer	1,000	800	100	750		Overtime	34
Fall	900	800	100	750		Subcontracting	60
Winter	1,200	800	100	750		Holding cost	5
						Shortage cost	Not allowed
						Initial Inventory	25

The solution screen is displayed next. The window on the left contains the production quantities as expressed in transportation form. The window on the right summarizes the production quantities, unit-months of holding (and shortage if applicable), and the costs.

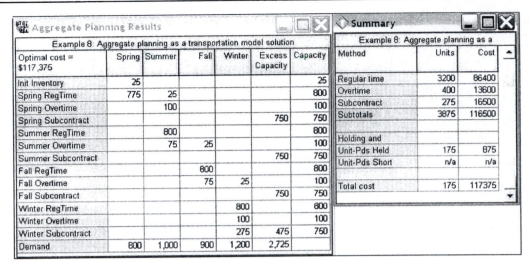

It is even more obvious that this is a transportation problem if the second window of output is examined, which is the transportation model itself.

Transportation Model

Example 8: Aggregate planning as a transportation model solution

	Spring	Summer	Fall	Winter	Capacity
Init Inventory	0	5	10	15	25
Spring RegTime	27	32	37	42	800
Spring Overtime	34	39	44	49	100
Spring Subcontract	60	65	70	75	750
Summer RegTime	9,999	27	32	37	800
Summer Overtime	9,999	34	39	44	100
Summer Subcontract	9,999	60	65	70	750
Fall RegTime	9,999	9,999	27	32	800
Fall Overtime	9,999	9,999	34	39	100
Fall Subcontract	9,999	9,999	60	65	750
Winter RegTime	9,999	9,999	9,999	27	800
Winter Overtime	9,999	9,999	9,999	34	100
Winter Subcontract	9,999	9,999	9,999	60	750
Demand	800	1,000	900	1,200	2,725

The large numbers (9999) have been entered in order to preclude the program from backordering. If you like, this table could be copied; you could then open the transportation model, create a new empty table that is 13 by 4 and paste this data into that table.

 **Assembly-Line Balancing**

This model is used to balance workloads on an assembly line. Five heuristic rules can be used for performing the balance. The cycle time can be given explicitly or the production rate can be given and the program will compute the cycle time. This model will not split tasks. Task splitting is discussed in detail in a later section.

The Model

The general framework for assembly-line balancing is dictated by the number of tasks that are to be balanced. These tasks are partially ordered, as shown, for example in the precedence diagram that follows.

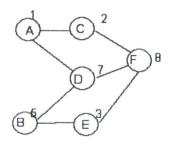

Method		Cycle time computation		Task time unit		Instruction
Longest operation time ▼		⦿ Given ◯ Computed	10	seconds ▼		Enter the va

Example 1 - Cycle time given							
TASK	Seconds	Predecessor 1	Predecessor 2	Predecessor 3	Predecessor 4	Predecessor 5	Predecessor 6
a	1						
b	5						
c	2	a					
d	7	A	b				
e	3	b					
f	8	c	d	e			

Method. The five heuristic rules that can be chosen are as follows:

1. Longest operation time
2. Most following tasks
3. Ranked positional weight
4. Shortest operation time
5. Least number of following tasks

NOTE: Ties are broken in an arbitrary fashion if two tasks have the same priority based on the rule given. Note that tie-breaking can affect the final results.

The remaining parameters are as follows:

Cycle time computation. The cycle time can be given in one of two ways. The cycle time can be given directly (see Example 1) which is the easiest method or, the cycle time can be converted from the demand rate which more common. The cycle time is converted into the same units as the times for the tasks. (See Example 2.)

Task time unit. The time unit for the tasks is given by this drop-down box. You must choose either seconds, hours, or minutes. Notice that the column heading for the task times will change as you select different time units.

Task names. The task names are essential for assembly-line balancing because they determine the precedences. Case does not matter.

Task times. The task times are given.

Predecessors (precedences). Enter the predecessors, one per cell. If there are two predecessors they must be entered in two cells. Do not enter "*a, b.*" In fact, a comma will not be accepted. Notice that in the precedence list in the previous screen both *a* and *A* have been typed. As mentioned previously, the case of the letters is irrelevant.

Example 1

In this example there are six tasks, *a* through *f*. The precedence diagram for this problem appears previously. The time to perform each task is above the task. Also, note that the tasks that are ready at the beginning of the balance are tasks *a* and *b*. Finally, in this first example, we use a cycle time of 10.

Solution

The following screen contains the solution to the first example. The solution screen consists of two windows as shown below. The window on the left gives the complete results for the method chosen whereas the window on the right gives the number of stations required (not the theoretical number) when using each balancing rule. The solution screen will always have the same appearance and contain the same information regardless of the rule that is chosen for the balance. Also, as shown in the summary window on the right, in this case each rule leads to 3 stations. This is not always the case as is demonstrated later in this section.

Station numbers. The station numbers appear in the far left column. They are displayed only for the first task that is loaded into each station. In this example, three stations are required.

Assembly Line Balancing Results						Heuristic res...	
Example 1 - Cycle time given solution						Example 1 - Cycle time given solution	
Station	Task	Time (seconds)	Time left (seconds)	Ready tasks		Method	Number of stations
				a,b		Longest operation time	3
1	b	5	5	a,e		Most following tasks	3
	e	3	2	a		Ranked positional	3
	a	1		c,d		Shortest operation time	3
2	d	7	3	c		Fewest following tasks	3
	c	2		f			
3	f	8					
Summary Statistics							
Cycle time	10	seconds					
Min (theoretical) # of stations	3						
Actual # of stations	3						
Time allocated (cycle time * # stations)	30	seconds/cycle					
Time needed (sum of task times)	26	seconds/unit					
Idle time (allocated-needed)	4	seconds/cycle					
Efficiency (needed/allocated)	86.67%						
Balance Delay (1-efficiency)	13.33%						

Task names. The tasks that are loaded into the station are listed in the second column. In this example, Tasks *b, e,* and *a* are in Station 1; Tasks *d* and *c* are in Station 2; and Task *f* is in Station 3.

Task times. The length of time for each task appears in the third column.

Time left. The length of time that remains at the station is listed in the fourth column. The last number at each station is, of course, the idle time at that station. The idle times are colored in red. For example, there is 1 second of idle time at Station 1, 1 second at Station 2, and 2 seconds at Station 3, for a total of 4 seconds of idle time per cycle.

Ready tasks. The tasks that are ready appear here. A ready task is any task that has had its precedences met. This is emphasized because some books do not list a task as ready if its time exceeds the time remaining at the station. Also, if the number of characters in the ready task list is very long, you might want to widen that column.

Cycle time. The cycle time that was used appears below the balance. This cycle time was either given directly or computed. In this example, the cycle time was given directly as 10 seconds.

Time allocated. The total time allocated for making each unit is displayed. This time is the product of the number of stations and the cycle time at each station. In this example there are three stations, each with a cycle time of 10 seconds, for a total work time of 30 station-seconds.

The time needed to make one unit. This is simply the sum of the task times. In the example we have $1 + 5 + 2 + 7 + 3 + 8 = 26$ seconds.

Idle time. This is the time needed subtracted from the time allocated. This example has $30 - 26 = 4$, which matches the 4 seconds of the three tasks with idle times displayed in red.

Efficiency. Efficiency is defined as the time needed divided by the time allocated. In this example, the efficiency is computed as 26/30, which is .8667.

Balance delay. The balance delay is the percentage of wasted time or 100 percent minus the efficiency. In this example, it is 4 (the idle time)/30 or .1333, which is also determined by 1-.8667.

Minimum theoretical number of stations. This is the total time to make 1 unit divided by the cycle time and rounded *up* to the nearest integer. In this example, 26 seconds are required to make 1 unit divided by a 10-second cycle time for an answer of 2.6, which we round *up* to 3 stations.

In addition, a second window opens that displays the number of stations required using each of the different balancing rules. In this particular case, each rule led to the same number of stations, 3. This is not always the case as shown in Example 4.

The precedence graph can be displayed (see the end of this section), as well as a bar graph indicating how much time was used at each station. These are shown at the end of this section. In addition, if there is idle time at every station, a note will appear at the top indicating that the balance can be improved by reducing the cycle time. For example, because there are idle times of 1, 1, and 2 seconds at the three stations, we could reduce the cycle time by 1 second.

Example 2: Computing the cycle time

Suppose that for the same data, a production rate of 2250 units in 7.5 hours is required.

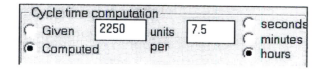

We assume full minutes and hours and compute the cycle time as follows:

(7.5 hrs/2,250 units)(60 min./hr.)(60 sec./min.) = 27,000/2,250 = 12 seconds

The solution screen follows.

Assembly Line Balancing Results ▬ ☐ ✖

Example 2 - Computing the cycle time solution

Station	Task	Time (seconds)	Time left (seconds)	Ready tasks
				a,b
1	b	5	7	a,e
	e	3	4	a
	a	1	3	c,d
	c	2		d
2	d	7		f
3	f	8		
Summary Statistics				
Cycle time		12	seconds	
Min (theoretical) # of stations		3		
Actual # of stations		3		
Time allocated (cycle time * # stations)		36	onds/cycle	
Time needed (sum of task times)		26	conds/unit	
Idle time (allocated-needed)		10	onds/cycle	
Efficiency (needed/allocated)	72.22%			
Balance Delay (1-efficiency)	27.78%			

Heuristic res ▬ ☐ ✖

Example 2 - Computing the cycle time

Method	Number of stations
Longest operation time	3
Most following tasks	3
Ranked positional weight	3
Shortest operation time	3
Fewest following tasks	3

Other Rules

Other rules that may be used are mentioned below, although the results are not displayed. Please note that this is one of the modules where if you change the method (using the drop-down box) from the solution screen, the problem will immediately be resolved. That is, you do not need to use the EDIT button and return to the data.

Most Following Tasks

A common way to choose tasks is by using the task with the most following tasks. Notice from the diagram that *a* and *b* each have 3 tasks following them. If *a* is scheduled first then the next choice is between *b* and *c* and *b* will be chosen since it has 3 tasks following rather than only 1 as c does. Similarly, If *b* is scheduled first then the next choice is between *a* and *e* and *a* will be chosen since it has 3 tasks following rather than only 1 as e does. The results display indicates the number of following tasks in the column named "ready tasks." This is displayed in the results screen for Example 4.

Ranked Positional Weight Method

The ranked positional weight computes the sum of the task and all tasks that follow. For example, for *a* the ranked positional weight is $1 + 2 + 7 + 8 = 18$, whereas for *b* the weight is $5 + 7 + 3 + 8 = 23$. The task with the largest weight is scheduled first (if it will fit in the remaining time). The results display indicates the ranked positional weight in the column named "ready tasks."

Shortest Operation Time

Another available rule is to give priority to the task that takes the least amount of time.

Least Number of Followers

The last rule that is available is the least number of followers.

Example 3: What to do if longest operation time will not fit

If the task with the longest time will not fit into a station, the task with the second longest time should be placed in the station, if it will fit, rather than opening a new station. Some books and software do not apply the longest operation time rule properly and open a new station rather than seeking a different, shorter task.

The following screen presents data for eight tasks. Notice that Tasks *b, c, e,* and *f immediately* follow Task *a*. (Task *d* follows but only after it follows Tasks *b* and *c*.)

Method	Cycle time computation		Task time unit	Instruction
Longest operation time	● Given 5 ○ Computed		seconds	Enter the name for this task. Almost

TASK	Seconds	Predecessor 1	Predecessor 2	Predecessor 3	Predecessor 4	Predecessor 5	Predecessor 6
				Example 3 - Proper application of longest operation time			
a	1						
b	5	a					
c	4	a					
d	2	b	c				
e	3	a					
f	1	a					
g	3	d	e	f			
h	3	g					

The balance appears in the following screen for a cycle time of 5 seconds. After Task *a* is completed, Tasks *b, c, e,* and *f* are ready. Task *b* is longest but will not fit in the 4 seconds that remain at station 1. Therefore, Task *c* is inserted into the balance. If the answer in your book differs from the program, you should check if the book has neglected to put in the task with the longest operation time that will fit.

Assembly Line Balancing Results					
Example 3 - Proper application of longest operation time solution					
Station	Task	Time (seconds)	Time left (seconds)	Ready tasks	
				a	
1	a	1	4	b, c, e, f	
	c	4		b, e, f	
2	b	5		e, f, d	
3	e	3	2	f, d	
	d	2		f	
4	f	1	4	g	
	g	3		h	
5	h	3			
Summary Statistics					
Cycle time	5	seconds			
Min (theoretical) # of stations	5				
Actual # of stations	5				
Time allocated (cycle time * # stations)	25	seconds/cycle			
Time needed (sum of task times)	22	seconds/unit			
Idle time (allocated-needed)	3	seconds/cycle			
Efficiency (needed/allocated)	88%				
Balance Delay (1-efficiency)	12%				

Example 4: Splitting tasks

If the cycle time is less than the amount of time to perform a specific task, there is a problem. We perform what is termed task splitting but which in reality is actually duplication. For example, suppose that the cycle time is 2 minutes and a task takes 5 minutes. The task is thus performed three times (by three people at three machines independent of one another). The effect is that 3 units will be done every 5 minutes, which is equivalent to 1 unit every 1.33 minutes, which fits into the 2-minute cycle.

Now, the actual way that the three people work may vary. Although other programs will split tasks, the assumptions vary from program to program. Rather than making assumptions, we leave it to you to split the tasks by dividing the task time appropriately.

Suppose that in Example 1 a cycle time of 5 seconds is used. Then it is necessary to replicate both Tasks *d* and *f* because they will not fit in the cycle time. The approach to use is to solve the problem by dividing the task times by 2, because this replication is needed. The results are presented in the following screen. Notice that different rules lead to different minimum numbers of stations!

Assembly Line Balancing Results

Example 4 - splitting tasks solution

Station	Task	Time (seconds)	Time left (seconds)	Ready tasks (# followers)
1	a	1	4	b(2),c(1),d(1)
	c	2		b(2),d(1)
2	b	5		d(1),e(1)
3	d	3.5		e(1)
4	e	3		f(0)
5	f	4		

Summary Statistics		
Cycle time	5	seconds
Min (theoretical) # of stations	4	
Actual # of stations	5	
Time allocated (cycle time * # stations)	25	onds/cycle
Time needed (sum of task times)	18.5	conds/unit
Idle time (allocated-needed)	6.5	onds/cycle
Efficiency (needed/allocated)	74%	
Balance Delay (1-efficiency)	26%	

Heuristic res...

Example 4 - splitting tasks solution

Method	Number of stations
Longest operation time	5
Most following tasks	5
Ranked positional weight	4
Shortest operation time	5
Fewest following tasks	5

Graphs

Two different graphs are available. The first is a precedence graph, as shown in the following figure. Please note that there may be several different ways to draw a precedence graph.

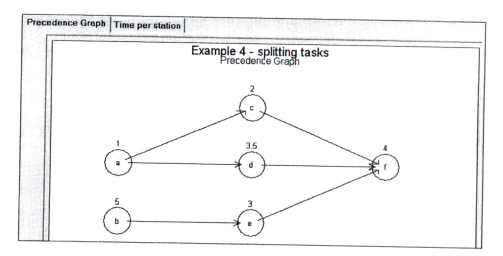

Example 4 - splitting tasks
Precedence Graph

The second graph (not displayed here) is of time used at each station. In a perfect world these would all be the same (a perfect balance).

The Assignment Model

The assignment model is used to solve the traditional one-to-one assignment problem of assigning employees to jobs, employees to machines, machines to jobs, and so on. The model is a special case of the transportation method. In order to generate an assignment problem, it is necessary to provide the number of jobs and machines and to indicate whether the problem is a minimization or maximization problem. The number of jobs and number of machines do not have to be equal but usually they are.

Objective function. The objective can be to minimize or to maximize. This is set at the creation screen but can be changed in the data screen.

Example

The following table shows data for a 7-by-7 assignment problem. The goal is to assign each salesperson to a territory at minimum total cost. There must be exactly one salesperson per territory and exactly one territory per salesperson.

	Mort	Cippy	Bruce	Beth	Lauren	Eddie	Brian
Pennsylvania	12	54	*	87	54	89	98
New Jersey	33	45	87	27	34	76	65
New York	12	54	76	23	87	44	62
Florida	15	37	37	65	26	96	23
Canada	42	32	18	77	23	55	87
Mexico	40	71	78	76	82	90	44
Europe	12	34	65	23	44	23	12

* Bruce is not allowed to work in the state of Pennsylvania.

The data structure is nearly identical to the structure for the transportation model. The basic difference is that the assignment model does not display supplies and demands because they are all equal to one.

NOTE: To try to preclude an assignment from being made, such as Bruce to Pennsylvania in this example, enter a very large cost. If you type '**x**', the program will place a cost of 9,999 for minimization problems or a profit of -9,999 for maximization problems in that cell.

The Solution

Assignments. The "Assigns" in the main body of the table are the assignments that are to be made. In the example, Mort is to be assigned to Pennsylvania, Cippy to Florida, Bruce to Canada, Beth to New York, Lauren to New Jersey, Eddie to Europe, and Brian to Mexico.

Total cost. The total cost appears in the upper left cell, $191 in this example.

Assignment Example Solution							
Optimal cost = $191	Mort	Cippy	Bruce	Beth	Lauren	Eddie	Brian
Pennsylvania	Assign 12	54	9,999	87	54	89	98
New Jersey	33	45	87	27	Assign 34	76	65
New York	12	54	76	Assign 23	87	44	62
Florida	15	Assign 37	37	65	26	96	23
Canada	42	32	Assign 18	77	23	56	87
Mexico	58	71	78	76	82	90	Assign 44
Europe	12	34	65	23	44	Assign 23	12

The assignments can also be given in list form, as shown in the following screen.

Assignment Example Solution		
JOB	Assigned to	Cost
Pennsylvania	Mort	12
New Jersey	Lauren	34
New York	Beth	23
Florida	Cippy	37
Canada	Bruce	18
Mexico	Brian	44
Europe	Eddie	23
Total		191

The marginal costs can be displayed also. For example, if we want to assign Mort to New Jersey, the total will increase by $30 to $221.

Assignment Example Solution							
	Mort	Cippy	Bruce	Beth	Lauren	Eddie	Brian
Pennsylvania			9,945	51	11	32	58
New Jersey	30	0	42			28	34
New York	13	13	35		57		35
Florida	20			46		56	
Canada	66	14		77	16	35	83
Mexico	42	13	20	36	35	29	
Europe	34	14	45	21	35		6

Breakeven/Cost-Volume Analysis

Cost-volume analysis is used in several different areas of POM and QM, especially capacity planning and location analysis. (The location module includes breakeven analysis as one of its submodels.) Cost-volume analysis is used to find the point of indifference between two options based on fixed and variable costs. A breakeven point is computed in terms of units or dollars. Breakeven analysis is simply a special case of cost-volume analysis where there is one fixed cost, one variable cost, and a revenue per unit.

Cost-Volume Analysis

In cost-volume analysis two or more options are compared to determine what option is least costly at any volume. The costs consist of two types – fixed costs and variable costs, but there may be several individual costs that comprise the fixed costs or the variable costs. In the example that follows, there are five different individual costs and two options.

Volume for volume analysis		Instruction		
◄ [____] ►	250	This cell can not be changed.		

			Example 1 - Cost-volume example	
		Cost Type	Option 1	Option 2
Lease		Fixed	800	700
Salary		Fixed	500	200
Material		Variable	6	6
Labor		Variable	2	1
Utilities		Variable	2	5

Data

Cost type. Each type of cost must be identified as either a fixed cost or a variable cost. The default is that the first cost in the list is fixed and that all other costs are variable. These values can be changed by using the drop-down box in that cell.

Costs. The specific costs for each option are listed in the two right columns.

Volume. If a volume analysis is desired, enter the volume at which this analysis should be performed. The volume analysis will compute the total cost (revenue) at the chosen volume. If the volume is 0, a second volume analysis will not be performed other than for the breakeven point. Volume analysis for this example is at 250 units.

Solution

The solution screen is very straightforward. In the preceding screen there are five costs with some fixed and some variable. The program displays the following results:

Breakeven/Cost-Volume Analysis Results			
Example 1 - Cost-volume example solution			
	Cost Type	Option 1	Option 2
Lease	Fixed	800	700
Salary	Fixed	500	200
Material	Variable	6	6
Labor	Variable	2	1
Utilities	Variable	2	5
Total fixed costs		1,300	900
Total variable costs per unit		10	12
BREAKEVEN POINTS	Units	Dollars	
Option 1 vs Option 2	200	3,300	
Volume analysis @	250		
Total Fixed Costs		1,300	900
Total Variable Costs		2,500	3,000
Total Costs		3,800	3,900

Total fixed costs. For each of the two options, the program takes the fixed costs, sums them, and lists them in the table. In this example, the total fixed costs for Option 1 are $1300 (800+500), whereas the total fixed costs for Option 2 are $900 (700+200).

Total variable costs. The program identifies the variable costs, sums them, and lists them. In this example, the total variable costs for Option 1 are $10 per unit, whereas for Option 2 they are $12 per unit.

Breakeven point in units. The breakeven point is the difference between the fixed costs divided by the difference between the variable costs, and this is displayed in units. In the example, it is 200 units.

Breakeven point in dollars. The breakeven point can also be expressed in dollars.

A volume analysis has been performed for a volume of 250 units. The total fixed costs and total variable costs have been computed for each option and these have been summed to yield the total cost for each option.

A graph is available, as follows.

Example 1 - Cost-volume example

Example 2: Breakeven analysis

One standard type of breakeven analysis involves revenue versus costs.

	Cost Type	Costs	Revenues
		Example 2	
Fixed Costs	Fixed	10,000	xxxxxxx
Variable costs	Variable	20	xxxxxxx
Revenue per unit	Variable	xxxxxxx	25

Data entry for this option is slightly different in that the program creates a column for costs and a column for revenues. The fixed and variable costs get entered in the cost column and the revenue-per-unit is placed in the revenue column.

This model requires exactly three inputs. The first is for the fixed cost of $10,000, the second for the variable cost of $20 per unit, and the third for the (variable) revenue of $25 per unit. The program will compute a breakeven volume of 2000 units or $50,000 (not shown).

This example could also have been solved using the cost-volume submodel. Select two options and let one be the costs and one be the revenue. Place the fixed costs and variable costs in their obvious cells; use no fixed cost for the revenue and use the revenue per unit as a variable cost, displayed as follows.

	Cost Type	Costs	Revenues
		Example 2 - part b: Using cost-volume analysis for traditional breakeven	
Cost 1	Fixed	10,000	0
Cost 2	Variable	20	25

Example 3: Cost-volume model with more than two options

The cost -volume model can perform an analysis for up to five options. The output for a three-optioncost-volume analysis is demonstrated in the following screen. The solution screen indicates three breakeven points as it makes comparisons for Computer 1 versus Computer 2, Computer 1 versus Computer 3, and Computer 2 versus Computer 3. Of course, while there are three breakeven points, only two of them are relevant.

Breakeven/Cost-Volume Analysis Results

	Cost Type	Computer 1	Computer 2	Computer 3
		Example 3 - Three options solution		
Purchase	Fixed	1,000	1,500	3,000
Operate	Variable	.09	.07	.04
BREAKEVEN POINTS	Units	Dollars		
Computer 1 vs Computer 2	25,000	3,250		
Computer 1 vs Computer 3	40,000	4,600		
Computer 2 vs Computer 3	50,000	5,000		

This is seen a little more easily by looking at the following graph. The breakeven point at 40,000 units does not matter because at 40,000 units the two computers that break even (1 and 3) have higher costs than the Computer 2 option.

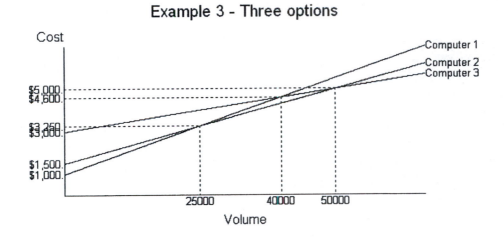

This is seen a little more easily by looking at the following graph. The breakeven point at 40,000 units does not matter because at 40,000 units the two computers that break even (1 and 3) have higher costs than the Computer 2 option.

Capital Investment

The capital investment module can be used for finding the net present value of a cash flow or for finding the internal rate of return of a cash flow. The data for this example consist of a stream of inflows and a stream of outflows. In addition, for finding the net present value an interest rate must be given.

Net Present Value

Consider the following example. A company is going to purchase new equipment that costs $100,000. Because of the use of the new equipment, the company will experience savings over the next 6 years of $22,000; $25,000; $22,000; $21,000; $19,000; and $18,000. At the end of 6 years the company anticipates being able to salvage the machine for $25,000. The company would like to know the net present value using an interest rate of 10 percent. The data screen follows.

Method	Interest rate		Instruction
Net Present Value	◄	► 1	Enter the name for this period. Almost any character is permissible.

		Example	
Name	Inflow	Outflow	
Period 0	0	100,000	
Period 1	22,000	0	
Period 2	25,000	0	
Period 3	22,000	0	
Period 4	21,000	0	
Period 5	19,000	0	
Period 6	18,000	-25,000	

The screen has two columns for data. One column is labeled Inflow and the other column is labeled Outflow. At the time of problem creation, six was the number of periods chosen. The data table includes the six periods plus the current period (0). The purchase cost of $100,000 is an outflow that occurs at the beginning of the problem, so this is placed in the outflow for Period 0. The six savings in the second column are inflows, and they are placed in the inflow column for Periods 1 through 6. The salvage value could be handled two ways, and we have chosen the way that we think gives a better display. The salvage value of $25,000 could have been added to the inflow in Period 6. Instead, it is represented as a negative outflow. This keeps the meaning of the numbers clearer. The last item to be entered is the interest rate in the text box above the data. The results appear as follows.

Capital Investment Results ▭◻✕

Example Solution	Inflow	Outflow	PV Factor	PV Inflow	PV Outflow	PV (Inflow-Outflow)
Period 0	0	100,000	1	0	100,000	-100,000
Period 1	22,000	0	.9091	20,000	0	20,000
Period 2	25,000	0	.8264	20,661.16	0	20,661.16
Period 3	22,000	0	.7513	16,528.93	0	16,528.93
Period 4	21,000	0	.683	14,343.28	0	14,343.28
Period 5	19,000	0	.6209	11,797.5	0	11,797.5
Period 6	18,000	-25,000	.5645	10,160.53	-14,111.85	24,272.38
Total	127,000	75,000	5.3553	93,491.41	85,888.15	7,603.246

A column has been created that gives the present value factors for single payments. To the right of this, the inflows and outflows are multiplied by these present value factors, and the far right column contains the present values for the net inflow (inflow-outflow) on a period-by-period basis. The bottom row gives the totals for each column and the solution to the problem is a net present value of $7,603.25.

Internal Rate of Return

The computation of the internal rate of return is very simple. The data is set up the same way but the method box is changed from net present value to internal rate of return. The results appear as follows. The internal rate of return for the same data is 12.38 percent and, of course, the net present value (bottom right) when using this rate is $0.

Capital Investment Results ▭◻✕

Example	Inflow	Outflow	PV Factor	PV Inflow	PV Outflow	PV (Inflow-Outflow)
IRR	.1238					
Period 0	0	100,000	1	0	100,000	-100,000
Period 1	22,000	0	.8899	19,577.26	0	19,577.26
Period 2	25,000	0	.7919	19,796.95	0	19,796.95
Period 3	22,000	0	.7047	15,502.8	0	15,502.8
Period 4	21,000	0	.6271	13,168.49	0	13,168.49
Period 5	19,000	0	.558	10,602.28	0	10,602.28
Period 6	18,000	-25,000	.4966	8,938.143	-12,414.09	21,352.23
Total	127,000	75,000	5.0681	87,585.91	87,585.91	0

Decision Analysis

There are two very basic models used for decision analysis – decision tables and decision trees. This module contains a model for a general decision table; a model for entering a decision tree in tabular form; an exciting, new model with a graphical user interface for decision trees; and a model for creating a decision table for demand/supply or 1 period inventory situations.

The Decision Table Model

The decision table can be used to find the expected value, the maximin (minimax), and the maximax (minimin) when several decision options are available and there are several scenarios that might occur. In addition, the expected value under certainty, the expected value of perfect information, and the regret or opportunity cost can be computed.

The general framework for decision tables is given by the number of options (or alternatives) that are available to the decision maker and the number of scenarios (or states of nature) that might occur. In addition, the objective must be selected either to maximize profits or to minimize costs.

Scenario probabilities. For each scenario it is possible (but not required) to enter a probability. The expected value measures (expected monetary value, expected value under certainty, expected value of perfect information) require probabilities, whereas the maximin (minimax) and maximax (minimin) do not.

NOTE: If the probabilities are identical then simply enter "=" in one of the probability cells and the program will set them all equal.

Profits or costs. The profit (cost) for each combination of options and scenarios is to be given.

Hurwicz alpha. Above the data is a scrollbar/textbox combination for entering the value for the Hurwicz alpha. The Hurwicz value is used to give a weighted average of the best and worst outcomes for each strategy (row). This is not in every textbook.

Example 1: A decision table

The following example presents three decision options: (1) to subcontract, (2) to use overtime, or (3) to use part-time help. The possible scenarios (states of nature) are that demand will be low, normal, or high; or that there will be a strike or a work slowdown. The table contains profits as indicated. The first row in the table represents the probability that each of these states will occur. The remaining three rows represent the profit that we accrue if we make that decision and a particular state of nature occurs. For example, if overtime is selected and there is high demand, the profit will be 180.

Objective
(•) Profits (maximize)
( ) Costs (minimize)

Hurwicz Alpha
◄ [____] ► .4

Instruction
This cell can not be changed.

Example 1

	Low demand	Regular dem	High demand	Strike	Slowdwn
Probabilities	.2	.3	.25	.15	.1
Subcontract	100	120	140	120	130
Overtime	120	150	180	10	90
Parttime help	105	130	190	50	80

Solution

The results screen that follows contains both the data and the results for this 3-by-5 example.

Decision Table Results

Example 1 Solution

	Low demand	Regular dem	High demand	Strike	Slowdwn	EMV	Row Min	Row Max	Hurwicz
Probabilities	.2	.3	.25	.15	.1				
Subcontract	100	120	140	120	130	122	100	140	116
Overtime	120	150	180	10	90	124.5	10	180	78
Parttime help	105	130	190	50	80	123	50	190	106
					maximum	124.5	100	190	116
						Best EV	maximin	maximax	Best

The maximum expected monetary value is 124.5 given by Overtime
The maximin is 100 given by Subcontract
The maximax is 190 given by Parttime help

Expected values. The expected values for the options have been computed and appear in a column labeled "EMV" (expected monetary value), which has been appended to the right-hand side of the data table.

Row minimum. For each row, the minimum element in that row has been found and listed. This element is used to find the maximin or minimin.

Row maximum. For each row, the maximum element in that row has been found and listed. This number is used for determining the maximax or minimax.

Hurwicz. These represent 40 percent multiplied by the best outcome plus 60 percent multiplied by the worst outcome for each row. For example, for subcontracting the Hurwicz is

$$(.4 * 140) + (.6 * 100) = 116.$$

Maximum expected value. Because this is a profit problem, finding the maximum values is of particular interest. The maximum expected value is the largest number in the expected value column, which in this example is 124.5.

Maximin. The maximin is the largest (MAXImum) number in the MINimum column. In this example, the maximin is 100.

Maximax. The maximax is the largest value in the table or the largest value in the maximum column. In this example, it is 190.

Perfect Information

A second screen of results presents the computations for the expected value of perfect information as follows.

Perfect Information						
Example 1 Solution						
	Low demand	Regular dem	High demand	Strike	Slowdwn	Maximum
Probabilities	.2	.3	.25	.15	.1	
Subcontract	100	120	140	120	130	
Overtime	120	150	180	10	90	
Parttime help	105	130	190	50	80	
Perfect Information	120	150	190	120	130	
Perfect*probability	24	45	47.5	18	13	147.5
Best Expected Value						124.5
Exp Value of Perfect Info						23

Perfect information. An extra row labeled "Perfect Information" has been added below the original data. In this row, the best outcome for each column is listed. For example, for the low demand scenario the best outcome is the 120 given by using overtime.

*Perfect*probability (expected value under certainty).* The expected value under certainty is computed as the sum of the products of the probabilities multiplied by the best outcomes. In the example, this is

$$EV(Certainty) = (.2*120) + (.3*150) + (.25*190) + (.15*120) + (.1*130) = 147.50$$

The row displays the individual multiplications in the preceding equation (24, 45, 47.5, 18, 13), and the sum (147.5) is displayed on the right-hand side of both the equation and the row.

Expected value of perfect information. The expected value of perfect information (EVPI) is the difference between the best expected value (124.5) and the expected value under certainty (147.5), which in this example is 23.

Regret/Opportunity Loss

A third available output display is that of regret or opportunity loss as follows.

Table values. The values in the table are for each column computed as the cell value subtracted from the best value in the column in the data. For example, under low demand the best outcome is 120. If we subcontract and get 100 the regret is 20 but if we use part time help the regret is 120 - 105 =15. The two columns on the right yield two sets of results. In the column labeled "Maximum regret", we determine the worst (highest) regret for each decision and then find the minimax regret (50) by looking at the best (lowest) of these regrets. In the column labeled "Expected Regret", simply multiply the regrets in each row by the corresponding probabilities in the top row.

Regret or Opportunity Loss							
Example 1 Solution							
	Low demand Regret	Regular dem Regret	High demand Regret	Strike Regret	Slowdwn Regret	Maximum Regret	Expected Regret
Probabilities	.2	.3	.25	.15	.1		
Subcontract	20	30	50	0	0	50	25.5
Overtime	0	0	10	110	40	110	23
Parttime help	15	20	0	70	50	70	24.5
Minimax regret						50	

There also is a window (not displayed in this manual) that yields Hurwicz values for alpha ranging from 0 to 1 by .01 for each decision option.

Decision Trees

Decision trees are used when sequences of decisions are to be made. The trees consist of branches that connect either decision points, points representing chance, or final outcomes. The probabilities and profits or costs are entered, and the decisions that should be made and the values of each node are computed. All decision tables can be put in the form of a decision tree. The converse is not true.

NOTE: Version 3 of the software includes two different input styles for decision trees. The first model has tabular data entry whereas the second model is easier to use because it has graphical data entry. The first model has been maintained in the software for consistency with previous versions.

Example 2: A decision tree – tabular data entry

The general framework for decision trees is given by the number of branches or the number of nodes in the tree. The number of branches is always one less than the number of nodes. Each node always has exactly one branch going into it. The number of branches going out of any node can be 0,1, or 2, . . . The nodes are of three types. There are decision nodes, chance nodes, and final nodes. Typically, the decision nodes are represented by rectangles, and the chance nodes are represented by circles. The following example shows a typical decision tree diagram. The figure has 12 branches. Profits are to the right of the terminal nodes. Notice that there is a $100 cost in the middle for selecting a certain (market research) branch.

In order to use the decision tree module, two things must occur. First, nodes must be added to the right of the ending branches. (Technically, it is illegal to draw a tree that ends with branches rather than nodes.) Second, the nodes must be numbered. The figure that follows shows the added nodes and the fact that all nodes have been given numbers. The most convenient way to number the nodes is from left to right and top to bottom.

The initial data screen is generated by answering that there are 12 branches and that we wish to maximize profits. The following screen contains both the data and the solution.

Decision Tree Results								_ □ ✕
Example 2 - Decision Tree in tabular form solution								
	Start Node	End Node	Branch Probability	Profit	Branch Use	End node	Node Type	Node Value
Start	0	1	0	0		1	Decision	465
Branch 1	1	2	0	0		2	Chance	340
Branch 2	1	3	0	0	Always	3	Chance	465
Branch 3	2	4	.6	0		4	Decision	300
Branch 4	2	5	.4	400		5	Final	400
Branch 5	3	6	.7	0		6	Decision	450
Branch 6	3	7	.3	500		7	Final	500
Branch 7	4	8	0	300	Backwards	8	Final	300
Branch 8	4	9	0	200		9	Final	200
Branch 9	6	10	0	400		10	Final	400
Branch 10	6	11	0	-100	Possibly	11	Chance	550
Branch 11	11	12	.5	750		12	Final	750
Branch 12	11	13	.5	350		13	Final	350

For the branch used columns the meanings are as follows:
Always - these are branches that should always be included
Possibly - these are branches that should be included if you get there and you MIGHT get there.
Backwards - these are branches that should be used if you get there BUT you should NOT get there.
(They are used for the backwards pass from right to left).

Start and end node. Branches are characterized by their start and end nodes. An added branch named "Start" appears in order to represent the final outcome. The node values are shown in the far right column. In this example, the value of the decision tree is $465.

Branching probabilities. These occur in column 4 and are the probabilities of going from the start node on the branch to the end node. The probabilities out of an individual chance branch should sum to 1.

Profits or costs. The profit (cost) for each ending node that is terminal is to be entered. In addition, it is possible to enter a profit or cost for any branch. For example, notice that in branch 10 (node 6 to node 11) we have entered a cost of $100 by placing "-100" (minus 100) in that cell.

The Decision Tree Solution

The solution values are as follows:

Branch use. For those branches that are decision branches and should always be chosen, an "Always" is displayed. In the example, choose node 1 to node 3 rather than node 1 to node 2. For those branches that are chosen *if we get there*, "Possibly" is displayed. For example, if we get to node 6 we should select node 6 to node 9 rather than node 6 to node 8. However, there is no guarantee that we will get to node 6 due to the probabilistic nature of the decision tree. The last type of branch is one that we should select if we get there, *but we should not get there*. These are marked as "Backwards." Look at branch 7 (node 4 to node 8). If we get to node 8, we should use this branch. However, since we will select node 1 to node 3 at the beginning, we should not end up at node 4.

Ending node. The ending node is repeated to make the output easier to read.

Ending node type. For each ending node, the program identifies it as either a final node, a decision node, or a chance node.

Expected value. The expected value for each node is listed. For final nodes, the expected value is identical to the input. For chance nodes, the expected value is the weighted combination of the values of the nodes that follow. For decision nodes, the expected value is the best value available from that branch. Both chance nodes and decision nodes will have any costs subtracted from the node values. For example, the value of node 11 is $550. However, the value of node 6 is $450 because of the $100 cost of going from node 6 to node 9.

A graph of the tree structure can be displayed by the program.

Example 2 - Decision Tree in tabular form
Network graph

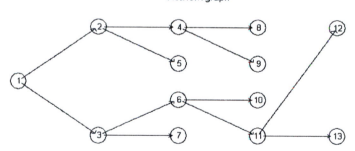

Example 3: A decision tree – graphical user interface

One of the models allows for decision trees to be entered graphically rather than in the table as given above. We will use this model to examine the same example just completed.

After selecting the model, the interface will be displayed as follows. This is the only model in the software that has an input interface that is not the usual data table.

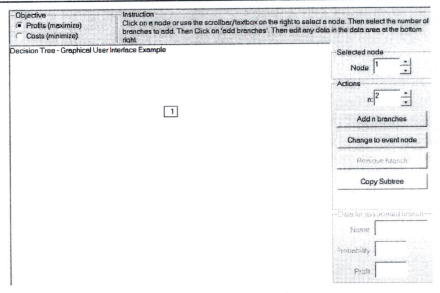

The graph is displayed in the large area on the left and created using the tools on the right. In the beginning, there is only one node. The next step is to add two event nodes to node 1. The tool on the right is set to node 1. The default for node 1 is that it is a decision node as needed in this case. A button is available to change the node if this becomes necessary. Because the default number of branches to add is 2, the first step is to click on the "Add n branches" button. The new tree appears as follows.

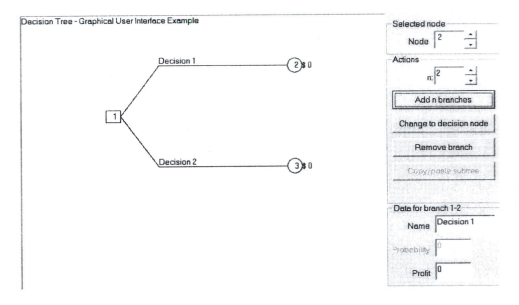

Notice that two branches have been added. The current node is node 2, which is indicated by both the fact that the node number in the upper right is node 2 and by the fact that the branch to node 2 is highlighted in a different color. Notice that the branches have been given default names of "Decision 1" and "Decision 2." These can be changed by using the branch information area at the bottom of the input tool area. At this point, two branches need to be added to node 2. The default is to add decision branches to events and vice versa. The type of node can always be changed later. Click on "Add n branches," then enter the probabilities for both new nodes and enter the profit of $400 for the second node. Then add two branches to node 3 and fill in the probabilities and the $500 profit. This yields the following diagram.

NOTE: Nodes may be selected by either clicking on them or using the scrollbar/textbox combination at the top of the tools section on the right.

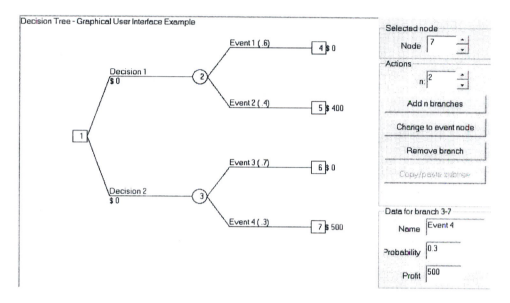

Complete the data input by adding decision branches and data at nodes 4 and 6 and an event at node 11. Also, include the $100 cost at decision 6 (node 6 to node 11). After all data have been entered, click on the Solve button on the toolbar. On the screen the data is in black and the solution is in blue as usual. In addition, the branches that should be used are indicated in blue.

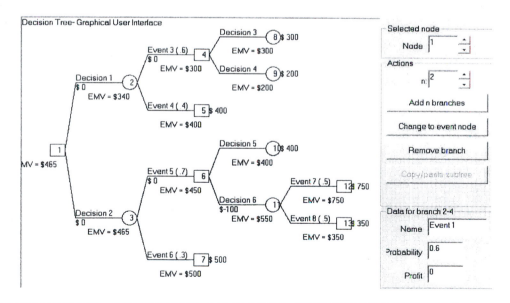

Example 4: Single period inventory

This model can be used to create a decision table for single-period inventory (supply/demand) situations. Consider the following example. In the past, an airline has observed a demand for meals that are sold on a particular flight as given in the following table. Each meal costs the airline $4 and sells for $10. If the airline is short a meal, it gives the passengers a voucher worth $5 for food at the airport of arrival. How many meals should the airplane stock per flight?

Meals	Probability
10	.1
15	.2
20	.5
25	.15
30	.05

Begin, by creating a table with 5 demands.

	Example 4 - Single Period Inventory (Supply/Demand)	
	Parameter	Value
Profit per unit	6	xxxxxxx
Profit per unit EXCESS	-4	xxxxxxx
Profit per unit SHORT	-5	xxxxxxx
Probability Distribution	Demand	Probability
Value 1	10	.1
Value 2	15	.2
Value 3	20	.5
Value 4	25	.15
Value 5	30	.05

The program is requesting three profits as well as the obvious demands and probabilities.

Profit per unit. This is the normal profit for units bought and sold. In this case the profit is, $10 - $4 = $6.

Profit per unit excess. This is the profit for units that are overordered. In some cases, where there is a salvage value that exceeds the cost of the unit this will be a profit whereas in other cases, this will be a loss. In this case there is a loss which is equal to the cost of an unsold meal, $4. This is a loss so -4 (minus 4) is entered.

Profit per unit short. This is the profit for units when the order is insufficient to meet the demand. It will be a profit if units to sell can be purchased after the fact at a cost less than the selling price. Otherwise, it will be a 0 or possibly a loss. In this case, a voucher is given, the loss is equal to the cost of the voucher, -$5. If the voucher were not given, there would be no profit or loss for units for which we could not satisfy the demand.

Demands and probabilities. Enter the list of demands and their associated probabilities.

The solution follows.. The airline should order 20 meals to maximize its expected profit. The value of the expected profit is $93.75.

Decision Table Results

	Demand=10	Demand=15	Demand=20	Demand=25	Demand=30	EMV	Row Min	Row Max
Example 4 - Single Period Inventory (Supply/Demand) Solution								
	.1	.2	.5	.15	.05			
Order 10	60	35	10	-15	-40	13.75	-40	60
Order 15	40	90	65	40	15	61.25	15	90
Order 20	20	70	120	95	70	93.75	20	120
Order 25	0	50	100	150	125	88.75	0	150
Order 30	-20	30	80	130	180	72.5	-20	180
					maximum	93.75	20	180
						Best EV	maximin	maximax

The maximum expected monetary value is 93.75 given by Order 20
The maximin is 20 given by Order 20
The maximax is 180 given by Order 30

 **Forecasting**

Forecasting models are divided into four submodels. The first type of model is when past data (sales) are used to predict the future (demand). This is termed time series analysis, and includes the naive method, moving averages, weighted moving averages, exponential smoothing, exponential smoothing with trend, trend analysis, linear regression, multiplicative decomposition, and additive decomposition.

The second model is for situations where one variable (demand) is a function of one or more other variables. This is termed (multiple) regression. There is overlap between the two models in that simple (one independent variable) linear regression can be performed with either of the two submodels.

In addition, this package contains a third model that enables the creation of forecasts given a particular regression model, and a fourth model that enables the computation of errors given demands and forecasts.

Time Series

The input to time series analysis is a series of numbers representing data over the most recent n time periods. Although the major result is always the forecast for the next period, additional results presented vary according to the technique that is chosen. For every technique, the output includes the sequence of "forecasts" that are made on past data and the forecast for the next period. When using trend analysis or seasonal decomposition, forecasts can be made for more than one period into the future.

The summary measures include the traditional error measures of bias (average error), mean squared error, standard error, mean absolute deviation (MAD), and mean absolute percent error (MAPE).

NOTE: Different authors compute the standard error in slightly different ways. That is, the denominator in the square root is given by n – 2 by some authors and n – 1 by others. *POM-QM for Windows* uses n – 2 in the denominator for simple cases and always displays the denominator in the output.

The Time Series Data Screen

Suppose that data is given as in the following table and the forecast the demand for the week of February 14 (and maybe the weeks of February 21, February 28, and so on) is needed.

Week	Sales
January 3	100
January 10	120
January 17	110
January 24	105
January 31	110
February 7	120

The general framework for time series forecasting is given by indicating the number of *past* data points. The preceding example has data for the past six periods (weeks), and the forecast for the next period – period 7 (February 14) is needed.

Method	# Periods to average	Instruction
Moving Averages	◄ [ ] ► 2	Enter the name for this column. Almost any character is permissible.

Example 1

	Demand(y)
January 3	100
January 10	120
January 17	110
January 24	105
January 31	110
February 7	120

Forecasting method. The drop-down method box contains the eight methods that were named at the beginning of this module and a method for users to enter their own forecasts in order to perform an error analysis. Of course, the results depend on the forecasting method chosen. A moving average is shown in the preceding screen.

Number of periods in the moving average, n. To use the moving average or weighted moving average, the number of periods in the average must be given. This is an integer between 1 and the number of time periods of data. In the preceding example, 2 periods were chosen, as seen in the extra data area.

Values for dependent (y) variable. These are the most important numbers because they represent the data. In most cases, these will simply be the past sales or demands. The data is in the demand column as 100, 120, 110, 105, 110, and 120.

Solution

The solution screens are all similar, but the exact output depends on the method chosen. For the smoothing techniques of moving averages (weighted or unweighted) and single exponential smoothing, there is one set of output, whereas for exponential smoothing with trend, there is a slightly different output display. For the regression models, there is another set of output. The first available method is the naive method which simply uses the data for the most recent period as the forecast for the next period. This is a special case of a moving average with n = 1 or exponential smoothing with $\alpha = 1$ so we do not display the naive method here. Begin with the moving averages.

Example 1: Moving averages

We are using a 2-week ($n = 2$) moving average. The main output is a summary table of results.

Example 1 Summary	
Measure	Value
Error Measures	
Bias (Mean Error)	1.25
MAD (Mean Absolute Deviation)	6.25
MSE (Mean Squared Error)	65.625
Standard Error (denom=n-2=2)	11.4564
MAPE (Mean Absolute Percent Error)	.0555
Forecast	
next period	115

The computations for all of these results can be seen on the following details window.

Example 1 Solution						
	Demand(y)	Forecast	Error	|Error|	Error^2	|Pct Error|
January 3	100					
January 10	120					
January 17	110	110	0	0	0	0
January 24	105	115	-10	10	100	.0952
January 31	110	107.5	2.5	2.5	6.25	.0227
February 7	120	107.5	12.5	12.5	156.25	.1042
TOTALS	665		5	25	262.5	.2221
AVERAGE	110.8333		1.25	6.25	65.625	.0555
Next period forecast		115	(Bias)	(MAD)	(MSE)	(MAPE)
				Std err	11.4564	

Forecasts. The first column of output data is the set of forecasts that would be made when using the technique. Notice that because this is a 2-week moving average, the first forecast cannot be made until the third week. This value is the 110, which appears as the first entry in the "Forecast" column. The 110 is computed as (100 +

120)/2. The following three numbers – 115, 107.5, and 107.5 – represent the "forecasts" of the old data; the last number in the column, 115, is marked as the forecast for the next period – period number 7.

Next period forecast. As mentioned in the previous paragraph, the last forecast is below the data and is the forecast for the next period; it is marked as such on the screen. In the example, it is 115.

Error. This column begins the error analysis. The difference between the forecast and the demand appears in this column. The first row to have an entry is the row in which the first forecast takes place. In this example, the first forecast occurs on January 17 (row 3) and the forecast was for 110, which means that the error was 0. In the next week the forecast was for 115, but the demand was only 105, so the error was -10 (minus 10).

Absolute value of the error. The fifth column contains the absolute value of the error and is used to compute the MAD, or total absolute deviation. Notice that the -10 in the error column has become a (plain, unsigned, positive) 10 in this column.

Error squared. The sixth column contains the square of each error in order to compute the mean squared error and standard error. The 10 has been squared and is listed as 100. Be aware that when squaring numbers it is quite possible that the numbers will become large and that the display of this column will become a little messy. This is especially true when printing.

Absolute percentage error. The seventh column contains the absolute value of the error divided by the demand. If the demand is 0, then the software will issue a warning regarding the MAPE.

Totals. The total for the demand and each of the four error columns appears in this row. This row contains the answers to problems in books that rely on the total absolute deviation rather than the mean absolute deviation. Books using total instead of mean should caution students about unfair comparisons when there are different numbers of periods in the error computation.

Averages. The averages for each of the four errors appear in this row. The average error is termed the *bias* and many books neglect this very useful error measure. The average absolute error is termed the MAD and appears in nearly every book because of its computational ease. The average squared error is termed the *mean squared error* (MSE) and is typically associated with regression/least squares. The average of the absolute percentage errors is termed the *mean absolute percentage error* (MAPE).

These four names are indicated on the screen as Bias, MAD, MSE, and MAPE underneath their values. In this example, the bias is 1.25, the MAD is 6.25, the MSE is 65.625, and the MAPE is 5.55 percent.

Standard error. One more error measure is important. This is the standard error. Different books have different formulas for the standard error. That is, some use $n-1$ in the denominator, and some use $n-2$. This program uses $n-2$. The denominator is displayed in the summary output as shown previously. In this example, the standard error is 11.4564.

NOTE: The normal distribution calculator can be used to find confidence intervals and address other probabilistic questions related to forecasting.

One more screen is available for all of these methods. It is a screen that gives the forecast control (tracking signals) results.

Control (Tracking Signal)

Example 1 Solution

	Demand(y)	Forecast	Error	RSFE	|RSFE|	Cum Abs	Cum MAD	Track Signal
January 3	100							
January 10	120							
January 17	110	110	0	0	0	0	0	0
January 24	105	115	-10	-10	10	10	5	-2
January 31	110	107.5	2.5	-7.5	2.5	12.5	4.1667	-1.8
February 7	120	107.5	12.5	5	12.5	25	6.25	.8

For moving averages there is a summary screen of error measures, versus the n in the moving average.

Errors as a function of n

Example 1 Solution

n	Bias	MAD	MSE	Standard error	MAPE
1	4	10	130	14.7196	.0868
2	1.25	6.25	65.625	11.4564	.0555
3	1.6667	6.1111	54.6296	12.8019	.0533
4	5	5	39.0625		.0421
5	11	11	121		.0917

One of the output displays (not shown in this manual) presents error measures as a function of n. Also, the moving average graph has a scrollbar that enables you to easily see how the forecasts change as n varies.

Example 2: Weighted moving averages

If the weighted moving average method is chosen, two new columns will appear on the data table as shown in the following screen. The far right column is where the weights are to be placed. The weights may be fractions that sum to 1 as in this example (.6 and .4), but they do not have to sum to 1. If they do not, they will be rescaled. For example, weights of 2 and 1 will be converted to 2/3 and 1/3. In this example, weights of .6 and .4 have been used to perform the forecasting. For example, the forecast for week 7 is $(.6 * 120) + (.4 * 110) = 116$.

Method	# Periods to average	Instruction
Weighted Moving Averages ▼	◄ ► 2	Enter the name for this column. Almost any character is permissible.

Example 2 - Weighted moving average

	Demand(y)		Past period	Weight	
jan 3	100		1 period ago	.6	
jan 10	120		2 periods ago	.4	
jan 17	110				
jan 24	105		.		
jan 31	110				
feb 7	120				

A (secondary) solution screen follows. As before, the errors and the error measures are computed.

Details and Error Analysis

Example 2 - Weighted moving average solution

	Demand(y)	Forecast	Error	|Error|	Error^2	|Pct Error|
jan 3	100					
jan 10	120					
jan 17	110	112	-2	2	4	.0182
jan 24	105	114	-9	9	81	.0857
jan 31	110	107	3	3	9	.0273
feb 7	120	108	12	12	144	.1
TOTALS	665		4	26	238	.2312
AVERAGE	110.8333		1	6.5	59.5	.0578
Next period forecast		116	(Bias)	(MAD)	(MSE)	(MAPE)
				Std err	10.9087	

Example 3: Exponential smoothing

Alpha for exponential smoothing. In order to use exponential smoothing, a value for the smoothing constant, alpha, must be entered. This number is between 0 and 1. At the top of the screen a scrollbar/textbox combination appears, enabling you to enter the value for the smoothing constant, alpha, as shown in the following screen. The smoothing constant alpha is .5 in this example.

NOTE: If you select alpha = 0, the software will find the best (lowest MAD) value for alpha!

Method	Alpha for smoothing	Instruction
Exponential Smoothing ▼	◄ || ► .5	Use the scroll bar or the text box to enter the alpha for smoothing. Set alpha to 0 in order for the program to find the value of alpha that minimizes the MAD.

Example 3 - Exponential Smoothing

	Demand(y)	Forecast
jan 3	100	0
jan 10	120	0
jan 17	110	0
jan 24	105	0
jan 31	110	0
feb 7	120	0

A starting forecast for exponential smoothing. In order to perform exponential smoothing, a starting forecast is necessary. When exponential smoothing is selected, the column label "Forecast" will appear on the screen. Underneath will be a blank column. If you want, you may enter one number in this column as the forecast. If you enter no number, the starting forecast is taken as the starting demand.

The results screen has the same columns and appearance as the previous two methods, as shown next.

Details and Error Analysis _ □ X

Example 3 - Exponential Smoothing Solution

	Demand(y)	Forecast	Error	|Error|	Error^2	|Pct Error|
jan 3	100					
jan 10	120	100	20	20	400	.1667
jan 17	110	110	0	0	0	0
jan 24	105	110	-5	5	25	.0476
jan 31	110	107.5	2.5	2.5	6.25	.0227
feb 7	120	108.75	11.25	11.25	126.5625	.0938
TOTALS	665		28.75	38.75	557.8125	.3308
AVERAGE	110.8333		5.75	7.75	111.5625	.0662
Next period forecast		114.375	(Bias)	(MAD)	(MSE)	(MAPE)
				Std err	13.6359	

One of the output displays (not shown in this manual) presents error measures as a function of alpha. Also, the graph for exponential smoothing has a scroll bar that enables you easily to see how the forecasts change as α varies.

Example 4: Exponential smoothing with trend

Exponential smoothing with trend requires two smoothing constants. A smoothing constant, beta, for the trend is added to the model.

Beta, for exponential smoothing. In order to perform exponential smoothing with trend, a smoothing constant must be given (in addition to alpha). If beta is 0, single exponential smoothing is performed. If beta is positive, exponential smoothing with trend is performed as shown.

Initial trend. In this model, the trend will be set to 0 unless it is initialized. It should be set for the same time period as the initial forecast.

Method	Alpha for smoothing	Beta for smoothing	
Exponential Smoothing with t ▾	◄ ► .5	◄ ► 5	Error analysis begins at first period with forecast. Please note that different authors use

Details and Error Analysis   _ ▢ ✕

Example 4 - Exponential Smoothing with trend solution

	Demand(y)	unadjusted forecast	trend	adjusted forecast	error	|Error|	Error^2	|Pct Error|
jan 3	100							
jan 10	120	110	5	100	20	20	400	.1667
jan 17	110	112.5	3.75	115	-5	5	25	.0455
jan 24	105	110.625	.9375	116.25	-11.25	11.25	126.5625	.1071
jan 31	110	110.7813	.5469	111.5625	-1.5625	1.5625	2.4414	.0142
feb 7	120	115.6641	2.7148	111.3281	8.6719	8.6719	75.2014	.0723
TOTALS	665				10.8594	46.4844	629.2053	.4057
AVERAGE	110.8333				2.1719	9.2969	125.8411	.0811
Next period forecast				118.3789	(Bias)	(MAD)	(MSE)	(MAPE)
						Std err	14.4822	

The solution screen for this technique is different from the screens for the previously described techniques. The forecast computations appear in the column labeled "unadjusted forecast." These numbers are the same as in the previous example (because the same value for alpha was used). The trend forecasts appear in the column labeled "trend." The trend is the difference between the doubly smoothed forecasts from period to period (weighted by beta). The forecasts appear in the column marked "adjusted forecast."

Note: Unfortunately, there are several different exponential smoothing with trend methods. Although they are all similar, the results will vary. Therefore, it is possible that the results given by *POM-QM for Windows* will not match the results of your text. This is unfortunate but unavoidable. If you are using a Prentice Hall text, be certain that the software is registered (**Help, User Information**) for that text in order to get the matching results.

Example 5: Trend analysis

As mentioned previously, the solution screen for regression differs from the solution screens for the other forecasting techniques. A sample summary output using regression for the same data follows.

Values for independent (x) variable. For time series regression, the default values are set to 1 through *n* and cannot be changed. For paired regression, the actual values of the dependent variable need to be entered (see Example 6).

Details and Error Analysis								
Example 5 - Trend analysis solution								
	Demand(y)	Time(x)	x^2	x * y	Forecast	Error	|Error|	Error^2	|Pct Error|
jan 3	100	1	1	100	106.1905	-6.1905	6.1905	38.3221	.0619
jan 10	120	2	4	240	108.0476	11.9524	11.9524	142.8593	.0996
jan 17	110	3	9	330	109.9048	.0952	.0952	.0091	.0009
jan 24	105	4	16	420	111.7619	-6.7619	6.7619	45.7233	.0644
jan 31	110	5	25	550	113.619	-3.619	3.619	13.0975	.0329
feb 7	120	6	36	720	115.4762	4.5238	4.5238	20.4649	.0377
TOTALS	665	21	91	2,360		0	33.1429	260.4762	.2974
AVERAGE	110.8333	3.5				0	5.5238	43.4127	.0496
Next period forecast					117.3333	(Bias)	(MAD)	(MSE)	(MAPE)
Intercept	104.3333						Std err	8.0696	
Slope	1.8571								

The screen is set up in order that the computations made for finding the slope and the intercept will be apparent. In order to find these values, it is necessary to compute the sum of the x^2 and the sum of the *xy*. These two columns are presented. Depending on the book, either the sum of these columns or the average of these columns, as well as the first two columns, will be used to generate the regression line. The line is given by the slope and the intercept, which are listed at the bottom left of the screen. In this example, the line that fits the data best is given by:

$$y = 104.33 + 1.857 * x$$

which is read as "Sales has a base of 104 with an increase of 1.857 per week."

If the data is sequential, the next period forecast is displayed. This is given by inserting one more than the number of periods into the regression line. In the example, we would insert 7 into the preceding equation, yielding 117.33, as shown on the screen at the bottom of the forecast column.

The standard error is computed and shown as with all other methods. In this example, it is 8.0696, which is better than any other method seen yet. Also notice that the mean squared error is displayed (43.41 in this example). The bias is, of course, 0, because linear regression is unbiased. The summary screen is displayed as follows.

Notice that the correlation coefficient and *r*-squared (r^2) coefficient are displayed as output. In the summary are the forecasts for the next several periods, because this was a trend analysis (time series regression).

Forecasting Results

Example 5 - Trend analysis summary			
Measure	Value	Future Period	Forecast
Error Measures		7	117.3333
Bias (Mean Error)	0	8	119.1905
MAD (Mean Absolute Deviation)	5.5238	9	121.0476
MSE (Mean Squared Error)	43.4127	10	122.9047
Standard Error (denom=n-2=4)	8.0696	11	124.7619
MAPE (Mean Absolute Percent Error)	.0496	12	126.619
Regression line		13	128.4762
Demand(y) = 104.3333		14	130.3333
+ 1.8571 * Time(x)		15	132.1904
Statistics		16	134.0476
Correlation coefficient	.4337	17	135.9047
Coefficient of determination (r^2)	.1881	18	137.7619
		19	139.619
		20	141.4761

The trend analysis graph has scrollbars that make it very easy to modify the slope and intercept of the line.

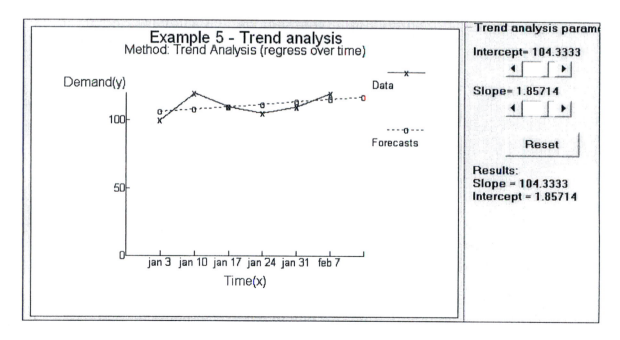

Example 6: Non time series regression

Regression can be used on data that is related. In the next screen, the sales of umbrellas as a function of the number of inches of rain in the last four quarters of the past year are presented. The interpretation of the solution screen is that the line that best fits this data is given by sales = 49.9389 + 27.4351 * number of inches of rain.

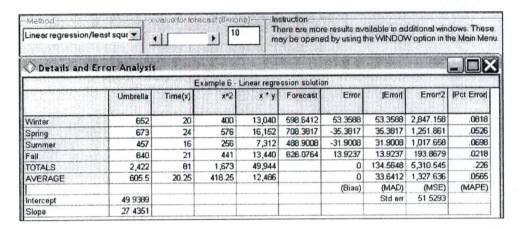

	Umbrella	Time(x)	x^2	x * y	Forecast	Error	|Error|	Error^2	|Pct Error|
Winter	652	20	400	13,040	598.6412	53.3588	53.3588	2,847.158	.0818
Spring	673	24	576	16,152	708.3817	-35.3817	35.3817	1,251.861	.0526
Summer	457	16	256	7,312	488.9008	-31.9008	31.9008	1,017.658	.0698
Fall	640	21	441	13,440	626.0764	13.9237	13.9237	193.8679	.0218
TOTALS	2,422	81	1,673	49,944		0	134.5648	5,310.545	.226
AVERAGE	605.5	20.25	418.25	12,486		0	33.6412	1,327.636	.0565
						(Bias)	(MAD)	(MSE)	(MAPE)
Intercept	49.9389						Std err	51.5293	
Slope	27.4351								

Above the data is a textbox that is used for a value for x to enter into the regression equation. The solution appears in the summary table (not displayed). In our example, if $x = 10$, then the summary table indicates that $y = 324$.

Example 7: Decomposition and deseasonalization

The following screen displays an example with seasonal data. As can be seen in the screen, there are 12 data points.

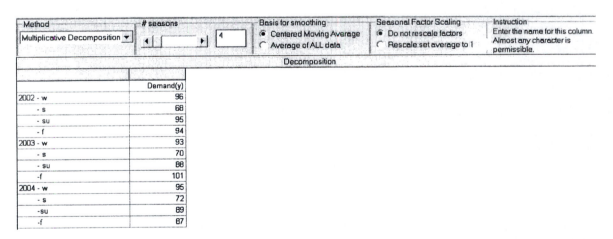

	Demand(y)
2002 - w	96
- s	68
- su	95
- f	94
2003 - w	93
- s	70
- su	88
-f	101
2004 - w	95
- s	72
-su	89
-f	87

You must enter the number of seasons, such as 4 quarters or 12 months or 5 or 7 days. In addition, you must enter the basis for smoothing. You may use either the centered moving average (which is common) or the average of all of the data. In addition, you can have the software scale the seasonal factors if you like.

The solution screen contains several columns.

Details and Error Analysis												_ □ ✕
Decomposition Solution												
	Demand(y)	time	CTD MA	RATIO	SEASONAL	SMOOTHED	Unadjusted forecast	Adjusted forecast	Error	|Error|	Error^2	|Pct Error|
2002 - w	96	1			1.0667	89.9993	88.6114	94.5196	1.4804	1.4804	2.1915	.0154
- s	68	2			.8132	83.6254	88.2814	71.786	-3.786	3.786	14.3338	.0657
- su	95	3	87.875	1.0811	1.0391	91.4232	87.9513	91.3923	3.6077	3.6077	13.0157	.038
- f	94	4	87.75	1.0712	1.1046	85.0966	87.6212	96.7887	-2.7887	2.7887	7.7768	.0297
2003 - w	93	5	87.125	1.0674	1.0667	87.1868	87.2911	93.1112	-.1112	.1112	.0124	.0012
- s	70	6	87.125	.8034	.8132	86.085	86.961	70.7124	-.7124	.7124	.5075	.0102
- su	88	7	88.25	.9972	1.0391	84.6867	86.6309	90.0203	-2.0203	2.0203	4.0815	.023
-f	101	8	88.75	1.138	1.1046	91.4336	86.3008	95.3302	5.6698	5.6698	32.1467	.0561
2004 - w	95	9	89.125	1.0659	1.0667	89.0618	85.9707	91.7029	3.2971	3.2971	10.8712	.0347
- s	72	10	87.5	.8229	.8132	88.5445	85.6407	69.6387	2.3613	2.3613	5.5757	.0328
-su	89	11			1.0391	85.6491	85.3106	88.6483	.3517	.3517	.1237	.004
-f	87	12			1.1046	78.7596	84.9805	93.8717	-6.8717	6.8717	47.2202	.079
TOTALS	1,048								.4778	33.0583	137.8566	.3796
AVERAGE	87.3333								.0398	2.7549	11.4881	.0316
Next period forecast								90.2945	(Bias)	(MAD)	(MSE)	(MAPE)
										Std err	4.7933	

Centered moving average. The data is smoothed using a moving average that is as long as the time period – 4 seasons. Because there are an even number of seasons, the weighted moving average consists of one-half of the end periods and all of the 3 middle periods. For example, for summer 2000, the weighted average is:

$$\{.5(96) + 68 + 95 + 94 + .5(93)\}/4 = 87.875$$

This average cannot be taken for the first $n/2$ periods and begins in Period 3.

Demand to moving average ratio. For all of the data points that have moving averages computed, the ratio of the actual data to the moving average is computed. For example, for summer 2002, the ratio is 95/87.875 = 1.0811.

Seasonal factors. The seasonal factors are computed as the average of all of the ratios. For example, the summer seasonal factor is the average of 1.0811 (summer 2002) and .997167 (summer 2003), which yields 1.0391, as shown for summer 2002, summer 2003, and summer 2004.

Seasonal factor scaling. The four seasonal factors are 1.0667, .8132, 1.0391, and 1.1046, which sum to 4.0236 (rather than 4). If we select the option in the area above the data to scale the factors then our seasonal factors will be rescaled (multiplied by 4/4.0236) and become 1.0604, .8084, 1.033, and 1.0982, respectively.

Smoothed data. The original data is divided by its seasonal factor in order to take out the seasonal affects and compute the smoothed data.

Unadjusted forecast. After smoothing the data the software finds the trend line for the smoothed data. This column represents the "forecasts" using this trend line. The trend line itself can be found on the summary results screen.

Adjusted forecast. The final column (before the error analysis) takes the forecasts from the trend line and then multiplies them by the appropriate seasonal factors. The errors are based on these adjusted forecasts versus the original data.

The summary table contains the forecasts for the coming periods.

Forecasting Results ▢☐◻✖

Decomposition Summary					
Measure	Value	Future Period	Unadjusted Forecast	Seasonal Factor	Adjusted Forecast
Error Measures		13	84.6504	1.0667	90.2945
Bias (Mean Error)	.0398	14	84.3203	.8132	68.5651
MAD (Mean Absolute Deviation)	2.7549	15	83.9902	1.0391	87.2763
MSE (Mean Squared Error)	11.4881	16	83.6601	1.1046	92.4132
Standard Error (denom=n-2-4=6)	4.7933	17	83.33	1.0667	88.8861
MAPE (Mean Absolute Percent Error)	.0316	18	83	.8132	67.4914
Regression line (unadjusted forecast)		19	82.6699	1.0391	85.9042
Demand(y) = 88.94153		20	82.3398	1.1046	90.9547
-.3301 * time		21	82.0097	1.0667	87.4777
Statistics		22	81.6796	.8132	66.4178
Correlation coefficient	.9488	23	81.3495	1.0391	84.5322
Coefficient of determination (r^2)	.9001	24	81.0194	1.1046	89.4962
		25	80.6893	1.0667	86.0693
		26	80.3593	.8132	65.3442

Additive Decomposition

The output is not displayed here. The additive model uses differences rather than ratios to determine the seasonal factors that are additive rather than multiplicative.

User Defined

The last method available is user defined. This allows you to enter the forecasts and let the software perform the error analysis. The same model is available as the fourth submodel when **New** is selected. This is exhibited in the last model of this section which is displayed on page 98.

Multiple Regression

As noted earlier, the forecasting module can perform multiple regression. There are two inputs to the data. The number of periods of data must be given; in addition, the number of independent variables must be given. In this example, we extend the regression problem in Example 6. Note that for simple regressions (one independent variable) there are two submodels that can be used to solve the problem: either time series analysis using the regression method or the regression submodel.

Example 8: Multiple Regression

In this example, two independent variables are used, therefore multiple regression must be used. We have entered 4 for the number of periods and 2 for the number of independent variables.

The data have been filed in and the solution screen appears next. The input has four columns: one for the name of the time period; one for the dependent variable, umbrellas; one for the independent variable, rain; and one for the independent variable, time (1 through 4). The output display is somewhat different from previous displays. The computations are *not* shown. The regression equation is not shown explicitly on this screen but can be found by looking at the beta coefficients below the table. That is, the equation is

$$\text{Umbrella sales} = 98.2381 + (26.5238 * \text{Rain}) - (11.9381 * \text{time}).$$

This is shown explicitly on the summary screen that we do not display.

Details and Error Analysis								
Example 8 - Multiple Regression Solution								
	Umbrella	rain	time	Forecast	Error	|Error|	Error^2	|Pct Error|
Winter	652	20	1	616.7762	35.2238	35.2238	1,240.717	.054
Spring	673	24	2	710.9333	-37.9333	37.9333	1,438.934	.0564
Summer	457	16	3	486.8048	-29.8048	29.8048	888.3248	.0652
Fall	640	21	4	607.4857	32.5143	32.5143	1,057.179	.0508
TOTALS	2,422	81	10		0	135.4762	4,625.155	.2264
AVERAGE	605.5	20.25	2.5		0	33.869	1,156.289	.0566
					(Bias)	(MAD)	(MSE)	(MAPE)
Betas	98.2381	26.5238	-11.9381			Std err	68.0085	

Projecting

The third model in forecasting allows us to take a regression equation and project it. Consider the following example.

Example 9 - Regression Projecting Solution				
	Coefficients	Forecast 1	Forecast 2	Forecast 3
Intercept	80	1	1	1
X 1	3	20	22	21
X 2	7	100	110	120
X 3	21	4	4	4
X 4	-6	3	3	3
X 5	2	18	18	18
Forecast		942	1,018	1,085

When the problem is created, indicate that there are five independent variables and that three forecasts should be created. The regression line is given by the first column ($Y = 80 + 3x_1 + 7x_2 + 21x_3 - 6x_4 + 2x_5$). The three columns contain the data for x_1 through x_5 for each of the three forecasts to be made. Row 1 contains a 1 because this is for the intercept. Finally, the bottom row contains the forecasts, which are 942, 1018, and 1085 for the three scenarios.

Error Analysis

The last model can be used to enter both forecasts and data in order to perform a complete error analysis. The error analysis is identical to the ones displayed previously. The difference is that the software allows the user to enter the forecast column rather than relying on one of the available methods.

Example 10 - Computing Errors Solution					
	Actual	Forecast	Error	|Error|	Error^2	|Pct Error|
Past period 1	83	70	13	13	169	.16
Past period 2	42	75	-33	33	1089	.79
Past period 3	58	65	-7	7	49	.12
Past period 4	71	60	11	11	121	.15
Past period 5	57	65	-8	8	64	.14
Past period 6	26	60	-34	34	1156	1.31
TOTALS	337		-58	106	2648	2.67
AVERAGE	56.17		-9.67	17.67	441.33	.44
			(Bias)	(MAD)	(MSE)	(MAPE)
				Std err	25.73	

 # Game Theory

A zero sum game is given by a table that gives the payoff to the row player (Player 1) from the column player (Player 2). The game table has one row for each of the row player's strategies and one column for each of the column player's strategies.

Consider the two-player game given by the following table:

Row/Column	Strategy 1	Strategy 2	Strategy 3	Strategy 4	Strategy 5
Strategy 1	10	-12	34	75	67
Strategy 2	38	57	96	28	-33

If the row player selects Strategy (row) 1 and the column player selects Strategy (column) 1, the column player pays the row player 10. If the row player selects Strategy 1 and the column player selects Strategy 2, the column player pays -12 or, in other words, the column player receives 12 from the row player. Row and column must each choose a strategy without knowing what the opponent has selected.

Sometimes the solution is for the players to always select one strategy (termed a *pure strategy*) and sometimes the solution is for the players to select their strategies randomly (termed a *mixed strategy*). In either case, this can be determined.

Solution to the Example

The solution for this example is displayed next.

Game Theory Results						_ □ ✕
			Example Solution			
	Col strat1	Col strat2	Col strat3	Col strat4	Col strat 5	Row Mix
Row strategy 1	10	-12	34	75	67	.5325
Row strategy 2	38	57	96	28	-33	.4675
Column Mix--->	0	.5917	0	0	.4083	
Value of game (to row)	20.2544					

Row should play the first strategy 53.25 percent of the time and the second strategy 46.75 percent of the time. Column should play the second strategy 59.17 percent of the time and the fifth strategy 40.83 percent of the time and never play Strategies 1,

3, or 4. If they follow these mixes, the (expected) value of the game is that column will pay row 20.2544. That is, if they played this game a large number of times following their optimal mixes, the payoffs would be -12, 67, 57, and -33, and would average 20.2544.

Maximin and Minimax

When examining games, begin by finding the maximin and minimax. To find the maximin for the row player, examine each row and find the worst (minimum) outcome. These appear in the column labeled "Row minimum" as -12 and -33 in the following figure. Then find the best of these, -12, which is the maximum of the minima or the maximin.

To find the minimax for the column player examine each column and find the worst (maximum because column is paying) payoff. These appear in the row labeled "Column Maximum" and are 38, 57, 96, 75, and 67. The minimax is the best (lowest) of these, or 38. The value of the game is between the maximin and minimax as appears in this game, with a value of 20.2544, which is between -12 and 38.

Maximin/Minimax							
Example Solution							
	Col strat1	Col strat2	Col strat3	Col strat4	Col strat 5	Row Minimum	Maximin
Row strategy 1	10	-12	34	75	67	-12	-12
Row strategy 2	38	57	96	28	-33	-33	
Column Maximum	38	57	96	75	67		
Minimax	38						
-12 <= value <=38							

Expected Values for Row

The following figure displays the computations (multiplications) performed to determine the expected value for each of row's strategies. Because row should use both strategies, the expected values are the same and match the expected value of the game.

Row's Expected Values						
Example Solution						
	Col mix 1 * cell payoff	Col mix 2 * cell payoff	Col mix 3 * cell payoff	Col mix 4 * cell payoff	Col mix 5 * cell payoff	Expected Value (row sum)
Column's Optimal Mix	0	5917	0	0	4083	
Row strategy 1	0	-7.1006	0	0	27.355	20.2544
Row strategy 2	0	33.7278	0	0	-13.4734	20.2544
Value of game (to row)						20.2544

Expected Values for Column

Similarly, if column plays Column 2 or 5, column will achieve the value of the game. However, if column selects Column 1, 3, or 4, then he or she will pay more than the value of the game as shown by the expected values in the following figure.

Column's Expected Values						
		Example Solution				
	Optimal Row Mix	Col strat1	Col strat2	Col strat3	Col strat4	Col strat 5
Row 1 mix * cell payoff	.5325	5.3254	-6.3905	18.1065	39.9408	35.6805
Row 2 mix * cell payoff	.4675	17.7633	26.645	44.8757	13.0888	-15.426
Expected Value (Col sum)		23.0888	20.2544	62.9823	53.0296	20.2544
Value of game (to row)	20.2544					

Graphs are available if either or both players have at most two strategies.

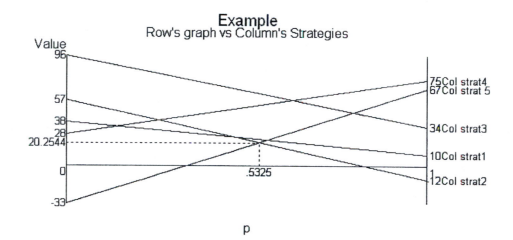

Goal Programming

Goal programming models are very similar to linear programming models, but whereas linear programs have one objective, goal programs can have several objectives. Consider the following example.

Example 1: Priorities

Suppose that a company manufactures two products ($x1$ and $x2$). The resource requirements and profit are provided in the following table.

	Product 1 ($x1$)	Product 2 ($x2$)	Available
Profit per unit	16	12	
Labor hours per unit	3	6	72
Material per unit	2	1	30

In addition, the company has the following goals:

1. The total profit should be at least 250.
2. It takes time to set up production for Product 2, so it should be produced in batches of at least 5.
3. The current demand for Product 1 is 14. Therefore, exactly 14 units should be produced.

This problem appears similar to a linear program, but now there are three goals rather than one objective.

Data

Any goal program is defined by the number of variables and the number of constraints or goals. Do not count the non-negativity restrictions as constraints. Thus, in this example, there are two variables and five constraints or goals (two constraints and three goals). The information is entered as shown in the following screen:

	Wt(d+)	Prty(d+)	Wt(d-)	Prty(d-)	X1	X2		RHS
Labor hours	0	0	0	0	3	6	<=	72
Materials	0	0	0	0	2	1	<=	30
Product 1 - demand	1	1	1	1	1	0	=	14
Profit	0	0	1	2	16	12	=	250
Product 2 - min batch size	0	0	1	3	0	1	=	5

Example 1: Goals ordered by priorities

Some of the information is identical to linear programming, but there are some differences. First, note that there is no objective function. Second, notice that there are four extra columns at the beginning (left) of the table before the decision variables. These extra columns are used for the goals and not for the constraints (where you can see that they are 0).

Goals/Constraints. In each line of the table, enter either a constraint or a goal. The first two lines represent constraints. Because these are constraints, the first four columns are not used (0s are entered). The constraints are entered in the usual fashion.

The next three lines represent goals, and there are two aspects to these goals. Because these are goals, notice that the sign in the row is "=". The values under $x1$ and $x2$ serve to create the goal in conjunction with the variables $d+$ and $d-$, indicating by how much we overachieve or underachieve the goal. For example, line 3 in the table stands for:

$x1 - (d1+) + (d1-) = 14.$

If $x1$ is below 14, $d1-$ represents the amount below, but if $x1$ is above 14, $d1+$ represents the amount over.

Similarly, the next line (Goal 4) represents

$16x1 + 12x2 - (d2+) + (d2-) = 270.$

Thus, $d2+$ and $d2-$ represent the amount of profit beyond 270 and below 270, respectively.

Mathematically, the goals are $d1+$, $d1-$, $d2+$, $d2-$, $d3+$, $d3-$. The question is: How do we want to order or weight these goals? That is, how do we contrast the importance of each of these six goals?

We do this using the priorities and weights on the line.

Priorities and weights: First, there are six goals ($d1+$, $d1-$, $d2+$, $d2-$, $d3+$, $d3-$) in this example, but it does not matter if our profit goal of 270 is overachieved, nor does it matter if more than five units of Product 2 are produced. Therefore, both the weights and priorities of these two goals have been set to 0. The priorities for the other four goals range from 1 to 3. The meaning of different priorities is the order in which the goals are satisfied. In other words, goals with Priority 1 must be satisfied before goals with Priority 2, which must be satisfied before goals with Priority 3, and so on. In this example, first try to make exactly 14 units of Product 1, then try to guarantee the minimum profit level of 270, then try to guarantee the minimum batch level of five for Product 2.

Within each priority, it is possible to assign different weights to the goals. This is shown in the next example.

The constraint sign. This is a drop-down box that can be used to change the constraint type from "less than or equal to" to "equal to" to "greater than or equal to." As stated previously, goals must have the sign "=".

Right-hand side coefficients. The values on the right-hand side of the constraints are entered here. For constraints, these are the usual coefficients, whereas for goals, these are the goals that are set.

The Solution

The following screen displays the summary solution (the simplex goal tableau is also available for display, as is a graph for two-dimensional problems).

Summary — □ X			
Example 1: Goals ordered by priorities solution			
Item			
Decision variable analysis	Value		
X1	14		
X2	2		
Priority analysis	Nonachievement		
Priority 1	0		
Priority 2	2		
Priority 3	3		
Constraint Analysis	RHS	d+ (row i)	d- (row i)
Labor hours	72	0	18
Materials	30	0	0
Product 1 - demand	14	0	0
Profit	250	0	2
Product 2 - min batch size	5	0	3

The optimal solution is to produce 14 units of Product 1 and 2 units of Product 2. Priority 1 will be achieved (the nonachievement is 0), whereas priorities 2 and 3 will not be achieved. Remember, $d+$ is the amount by which the goal is exceeded, and $d-$ is the amount by which it has come up short. The constraint analysis indicates that 18 fewer hours were used than were available, exactly the amount of material that we had was used, goal 3 was reached exactly, profit was underachieved (goal/constraint 4) by 22 and the batch size 3 (goal/constraint 5) was underachieved by 3.

Example 2: Using weights

We have revised our goal priorities as shown in the following example. This time meeting the profit level is the highest goal and everything else is secondary. However, we have given twice the weight to underachieving our five units of Product 2, compared with missing our goal of 14 for Product 1.

Example 2: Weighted goals								
	Wt(d+)	Prty(d+)	Wt(d-)	Prty(d-)	X1	X2		RHS
Labor hours	0	0	0	0	3	6	<=	72
Materials	0	0	0	0	2	1	<=	30
Product 1 - demand	1	2	1	2	1	0	=	14
Profit	0	0	1	1	16	12	=	250
Product 2 - min batch size	0	0	2	2	0	1	=	5

The results follow. Produce 12.5 units of Product 1 and 5 units of Product 2. Our first priority will be achieved but our second priority will not be achieved. (The 1.5 represents 14 - 12.5). Notice that there were only two priorities.

The goal/constraint analysis shows us that there are 4.5 labor hours left over, exactly the 30 pounds of available material are used, Product 1 demand is underachieved by 1.5, the profit goal is overachieved by 10, and the goal of making at least 5 units of Product 2 is met exactly.

Summary			
Example 2: Weighted goals solution			
Item			
Decision variable analysis	Value		
X1	12.5		
X2	5		
Priority analysis	Nonachievement		
Priority 1	0		
Priority 2	1.5		
Constraint Analysis	RHS	d+ (row i)	d- (row i)
Labor hours	72	0	4.5
Materials	30	0	0
Product 1 - demand	14	0	1.5
Profit	250	10	0
Product 2 - min batch size	5	0	0

Integer and Mixed Programming

Any integer or mixed integer linear program is defined by the number of variables and the number of constraints. As with linear programming, do not count the non-negativity restrictions as constraints since the program uses only non-negative variables must be non-negative.

Example 1: An all integer problem

Consider the following integer programming example:

maximize	$350x1$	$+ 500x2$		
subject to	$x1$	$+ 1.5x2$	$<=$	15
	$-x1$	$+ 4x2$	$>=$	0
	$x1, x2$	$>= 0$		
	$x1, x2$	integer		

The components and the data entry are nearly the same as for linear programming. The difference is that the input screen has one extra row for identifying the type of variable as either real, integer, or 0/1.

Objective	Maximum number of iterations	Maximum level (depth) in proced	Instruction
⦿ Maximize ◯ Minimize	◀ ▶ 100	◀ ▶ 50	This cell can not be changed.

Example 1: An integer program				
	X1	X2		RHS	Equation form
Maximize	350	500			Max 350X1 + 500X2
Constraint 1	1	1.5	<=	15	X1 + 1.5X2 <= 15
Constraint 2	-1	4	>=	0	- X1 + 4X2 >= 0
Variable type	Integer	Integer			

Objective function. The choice of minimization or maximization is made in the usual way at the time of problem creation, but it can be changed on the data screen using the objective option above the data.

Objective function coefficients. The coefficients (typically referred to as c_j) are entered as numerical values.

Constraint coefficients. The main body of information contains the constraint coefficients, which typically are called the $a_{ij}s$. These coefficients may be positive or negative.

The constraint sign. This can be entered in one of two ways. It is permissible to press the [<] key, the [>] key, or the [=] key. When you go to a cell with the constraint sign, a drop-down arrow appears in the cell and can be used.

Right-hand side coefficients. The values on the right-hand side of the constraints are entered here. These are also termed the $b_i s$. They must be non-negative.

The variable type. This is a drop-down box that will change the variable type from "integer" to "real" to "0/1." You can change all variables at once by clicking on the leftmost column. This is very useful for capital budgeting problems.

Maximum number of iterations and maximum level (depth).: If you receive a message regarding the number of iterations or depth rather than a solution, you may increase these numbers.

The Solution

The solution is given by a simple screen with the variables and their values.

Integer & Mixed Integer Programming ...		
Example 1: An integer program solution		
Variable	Type	Value
X1	Integer	9
X2	Integer	4
Solution value		5,150

Iterations

The iterations can be found in another screen. The LP solution to the original problem (see Iteration 1, Level 0) has $x1$ and $x2$ both as nonintegers. Branch on $x1$ by adding the constraint $x1 <= 10$. The LP solution to this problem has $x1$ as an integer but $x2$ is noninteger, so branch on $x2$ by adding the constraint ($x2 <= 3$). This yields an integer solution (iteration 3). Create the other branch by adding ($x2 >= 4$) and this yields an even better integer solution. Return to the original node and create the branch $x1 > 11$, which yields an infeasible solution. Therefore, the work is completed.

Iteration Results						
Example 1: An integer program solution						
Iteration	Level	Added constraint	Solution type	Solution Value	X1	X2
			Optimal	5,150	9	4
1	0		NONinteger	5,181.82	10.91	2.73
2	1	X1<= 10	NONinteger	5,166.67	10	3.33
3	2	X2<= 3	INTEGER	5,000	10	3
4	2	X2>= 4	INTEGER	5,150	9	4
5	1	X1>= 11	Infeasible			

A graph (not shown) is available for this module.

Example 2: A mixed integer program

Consider the following example:

$$\text{maximize} \quad 30x + 33y + 50z$$
$$\text{subject to} \quad 23x + 43y + 16z <= 1000$$
$$32x + 33y + 25z <= 2500$$
$$43x + 53y + 26z <= 1500$$
$$x, y, z >= 0$$
$$x \text{ integer,}$$
$$z \text{ 0/1}$$

This time use the extra row of information that needs to be given indicating the type of each variable (real, integer, or 0/1). The values are set by the drop-down boxes as displayed below. As mentioned previously, if you click on the cell at the lower left with "Variable type" in it, then it is possible to set all variables to the same type. That is, they may be all be set to be integer, all be set to be real or all be set to be 0/1 variables.

	x	y	z		RHS	Equation form
						Example 2: Mixed integer programming
	x	**y**	**z**		RHS	Equation form
Maximize	30	33	50			Max 30x + 33y + 50z
Constraint 1	23	43	16	<=	1,000	23x + 43y + 16z <= 1000
Constraint 2	32	33	25	<=	2,500	32x + 33y + 25z <= 2500
Constraint 3	43	53	26	<=	1,500	43x + 53y + 26z <= 1500
Variable type	Integer ▾	Real	0/1			
	Integer					
	Real					
	0/1					

The Solution

The variable types and their solution values are displayed.

Integer & Mixed Integer Programmi...		
Example 2: Mixed integer programming solution		
Variable	Type	Value
x	Integer	34
y	Real	.2264
z	0/1	1
Solution value		1,077.472

 **Inventory**

One type of inventory model uses different variations of the economic order quantity (EOQ) model in order to determine proper order or production quantities. Besides the standard EOQ model, included in the software is the economic production quantity (EPQ) model. For both the EOQ and EPQ model, shortages may be included. Finally, the software contains an EOQ model that allows quantity discounts.

A second, distinct type of model is ABC analysis.

The last two models are used for computing reorder points for normal distributions and discrete distributions.

EOQ-Type Models

The following screen contains an example that includes both the data and the solution.

Reorder point	Order Quantity (0=EOQ)	Instruction
○ No reorder point	◀ ▶ 20	There are more results available in additional windows. These
● Compute reorder point		may be opened by using the WINDOW option in the Main Menu.

Inventory Results

Example 1 Solution

Parameter	Value		Parameter	Results using EOQ	Results using 20
Demand rate(D)	200		Optimal order quantity (Q*)	16.3299	
Setup/Ordering cost(S)	20		Maximum Inventory Level (Imax)	16.3299	20
Holding cost(H)	30		Average inventory	8.165	10
Unit cost	0		Orders per period(year)	12.2475	10
Days per year (D/d)	250		Annual Setup cost	244.949	200
Daily demand rate	.8		Annual Holding cost	244.949	300
Lead time (in days)	5				
Safety stock	0		Unit costs (PD)	0	0
			Total Cost	489.8979	500
			Reorder point	4 units	

The Data

Demand rate. The rate of demand or usage is to be entered here. Typically, this demand rate is an annual rate, but it does not need to be. The time units for this demand rate must match the time units for the holding cost.

Setup cost. The setup cost is the fixed cost of placing each order or making each production run.

Holding cost rate. The holding cost rate is the cost of holding or carrying 1 unit of inventory for 1 time period. This cost is either given as a particular dollar amount or given as a percentage of the price of the item.

NOTE: If you want the holding cost to be a percentage of the unit cost, enter a percent sign, "%", after the number. For example, "20" means $20s, but "20%" means 20 percent of the unit cost. If the holding cost is a percentage of the unit cost, you must enter the unit cost.

Unit cost. This is sometimes necessary, but many times it is not because the EOQ is independent of the unit cost.

Reorder point. The option box above the data enables the calculation of the reorder point. Three lines of input are added in these cases. Ether enter a daily demand rate or enter the number of days in the year so that the daily demand rate can be computed from the annual demand rate. In addition, enter the number of days for the lead time.

Order quantity. Above the data is a textbox/scrollbar combination that allows you to enter a value for the order quantity. If you enter a number other than 0, two sets of results will be displayed. One column will be for the EOQ, whereas the other column will be for the specified order quantity.

The Solution

The output screen appears in the preceding screen where a standard EOQ model has been solved and, in addition, results determined when using an order quantity of 20 units. The model results are as follows:

Optimal order quantity. The optimal order quantity is the most economical order quantity. If there is no quantity discount, this is the EOQ. However, when a quantity discount is available (as in Example 3), this is either the EOQ or a discount point above the EOQ. In this example, the optimal order quantity is 16.33 units per order.

Maximum inventory level. It is useful to know the largest amount that will be in inventory. In the standard EOQ model, this is simply the amount that is ordered; in a production or shortage model, this is less. In this example, the inventory will never exceed 16.33 units when using the EOQ or 20 units if 20 is the order quantity.

Average inventory level. If there are no backorders, the average inventory is half of the maximum inventory. Annual holding costs are based on the average inventory.

Orders per year. The assumed time period is 1 year, and the number of orders is displayed. In this example, it is 12.25 for the EOQ and 10 for an order quantity of 20 units.

Unit costs. Unit cost is the total cost for ordering the units. In many instances, the individual unit cost will be 0, and, therefore, the total unit costs will be 0.

Total costs. The total cost of both the inventory costs and the unit costs is useful for checking work on problems with discounts.

Reorder point. The reorder point is the product of the daily demand rate and the number of lead time days. In this example, there is a daily demand rate of .8 units and a lead time of 5 days, which yields a reorder point of 4 units.

A graph of cost versus inventory is displayed next.

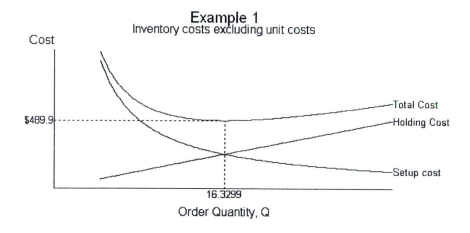

Example 2: Inventory with production

In the following example, data are displayed for a problem with production. The data includes the usual parameters of demand rate, setup cost, holding cost, and unit cost. Also displayed are results for a policy of producing 300 units per run. In this example the holding cost is set to 20% of the unit price. In addition, in this model, we are asked for a daily production rate and either a daily demand rate or the number of days per year. Notice in this example that the days per year is set to 250. The program computes the daily demand rate as 10,000/250. Alternatively, the daily demand rate could have been entered to compute the days per year.

Order Quantity (0=EOQ)		Instruction

300

Instruction: You may enter the DAILY demand rate directly or you may enter the number of days per year and the daily demand rate will be computed as d=D/days per year. Any non-negative value is permissible.

Example 2 - Production model with holding cost as a percentage

Parameter	Value
Demand rate(D)	10,000
Setup/Ordering cost(S)	25
Holding cost(H)	20%
Daily production rate(p)	80
Days per year(optional)	250
Daily demand rate(d)	0
Unit cost	90

The solution appears next. The daily demand rate has been found to be 40. The remaining results are the same as in the first example. Notice that the holding cost has been computed as $18 based on 20% of the $90 unit cost.

Inventory Results

Example 2 - Production model with holding cost as a percentage solution

Parameter	Value		Parameter	Results using EOQ	Results using 300
Demand rate(D)	10,000		Optimal production quantity (Q*)	235.7023	
Setup/Ordering cost(S)	25		Maximum Inventory Level (Imax)	117.8511	150
Holding cost(H)@20%	18		Average inventory	58.9256	75
Daily production rate(p)	80		Production runs per period (year)	42.4264	33.3333
Days per year (D/d)	250		Annual Setup cost	1,060.66	833.3333
Daily demand rate	40		Annual Holding cost	1,060.66	1,350
Unit cost	90				
			Unit costs (PD)	900,000	900,000
			Total Cost	902,121.3	902,183.3

Example 3: Quantity discounts

A screen for quantity discounts appears in the following illustration. The usual information is placed at the top. In addition, the number of price ranges must be given at the time of problem creation.

Inventory Results

Example 3: Quantity Discounts Solution

Parameter	Value				Parameter	Value
Demand rate(D)	100	xxxxxxx	xxxxxxx		Optimal order quantity (Q*)	24
Setup/Ordering cost(S)	40	xxxxxxx	xxxxxxx		Maximum Inventory Level	24
Holding cost(H)@20%		xxxxxxx	xxxxxxx		Average inventory	12
					Orders per period(year)	4.1667
	From	To	Price		Annual Setup cost	166.6667
Range 1	1	11	100		Annual Holding cost	235.2
Range 2	12	23	99			
Range 3	24	999,999	98		Unit costs (PD)	9,800
					Total Cost	10,201.87

A detailed analysis of the order quantities and costs at each price range is available, as follows.

Range	Quantity	Total Setup Cost	Total Holding Cost	Total Unit Cost	Total Cost
Details — Example 3: Quantity Discounts Solution					
1 to 11					
12 to 23	20.1008	198.9975	198.9975	9,900	10,298.0
24 to 999999	24	166.6667	235.2	9,800	10,201.87

Backorder Models

The software also has the capability to compute the EOQ or the production model with backorders. These models do not appear in all textbooks, so they are not displayed in this manual. If you have the software set for one of the Render texts these models will not show up in the model submenu.

ABC Analysis

The goal of ABC analysis is to identify the most important items that are kept in inventory. Importance is measured by dollar volume. An example appears as follows for a problem with six items.

Percent of items that are A items: 20
Percent of items that are B items: 30

Example 4: ABC Analysis

Item name	Demand	Unit price
Item 1	1,800	2
Item 2	340	4
Item 3	25	68
Item 4	870	2
Item 5	330	9
Item 6	50	3

For each item, the information to be entered is as follows:

Item name. As usual, a name can be entered on each line.

Demand. The demand rate for each item is to be given.

Unit price. The cost or price of each item is to be given

Percentage of A and B items. In the example, 20 percent of the items should be A items and 30 percent should be B items. After the program sorts the items by dollar volume, the first 20 percent of 6 items (.6 items rounded to 1) are classified as A items, and 30 percent of 6 (1.8 items rounded to 2) are classified as B items.

Inventory Results						
Example 4: ABC Analysis Solution						
Item name	Demand	Price	Dollar Volume	Percent of $-Vol	Cumulty $-vol %	Category
Item 1	1,800	2	3,600	31.25	31.25	A
Item 5	330	9	2,970	25.7813	57.0313	B
Item 4	870	2	1,740	15.1042	72.1354	B
Item 3	25	68	1,700	14.7569	86.8924	C
Item 2	340	4	1,360	11.8056	98.6979	C
Item 6	50	3	150	1.3021	100	C
TOTAL	3,415		11,520			

Notice that the items are sorted according to their dollar-volume percentages. That is, they do not appear in the same order as on the original screen of input. The output computed for each item is as follows:

Dollar-volume. This is the demand multiplied by the price for each item.

Dollar-volume percentage. This is the item dollar-volume divided by the total dollar volume.

Cumulative dollar-volume percentage. This is a running total of dollar volume when the items are sorted from highest dollar volume to lowest dollar volume.

Category. This is the classification explained previously.

Reorder Points for the normal distribution

Following is the solution screen for calculating the safety stock and reorder point for the case where demand during lead time is given by a normal distribution. The solution screen includes the input on the left.

Inventory Results

Example 5: Reorder points for the Normal distribution solution				
Parameter	Value		Parameter	Value
Daily demand (d-bar)	12		Z value	1.65
Demand Std dev (sigma-d)	2		Expected demand during lead time	36
Service Level %	95		Safety Stock	20.61
Lead time in days (L)	3		Reorder point	56.61
Lead time std dev (sigma L)	1			

Daily demand. This is the daily demand rate during the lead time.

Demand standard deviation. This is the standard deviation for the daily demand rate. If the daily demand rate is fixed, enter a standard deviation of 0.

Service level. This is the percentage of demands that should be met.

Lead time in days. This is the lead time in days.

Lead time standard deviation. This is the standard deviation of the lead time. If the lead time is fixed, enter 0 for the standard deviation.

NOTE: The display for Heizer/Render is based on a given lead time demand and standard deviation and has only three inputs. In general, to use the preceding display, if the problem has a given lead time demand and standard deviation, set the lead time days to 1 and the lead time standard deviation to 0.

Reorder Points for a Discrete Distribution

	Example 6: Reorder point - discrete distribution		
	Parameter	Value	
Reorder point w/o safety stock	70	xxxxxxx	
Carrying cost per year	7	xxxxxxx	
Stockout cost	18	xxxxxxx	
Orders per year	2	xxxxxxx	
Probability Distribution	Value	Probability	
Value 1	50	.1	
Value 2	60	.3	
Value 3	70	.25	
Value 4	80	.2	
Value 5	90	.15	

Reorder point w/o safety stock. This is the reorder point prior to consideration of safety stock. In this example, the initial plan is to reorder when the inventory falls to 70. Thus, if the demand during the lead time does not exceed 70, there will not be any stockouts. Because the maximum demand is 90 and the reorder point is 70 the maximum safety stock is 20 units.

Carrying cost per year. This is the usual cost of carrying inventory. In this example it is $7 per unit per year.

Stockout cost. This is the cost per unit of not being able to meet the demand. In this case it is $18 each time that we are short a unit.

Orders per year. This is the number of times per year the ordering process is performed. In this example, orders are placed twice a year.

Probability distribution. This is the column of lead time demands and their associated probabilities.

The results follow, indicating that the minimal cost safety stock is 10 and thus the revised reorder point is the original 70 plus the 10 for a total of 80 units.

Inventory Results				
Example 6: Reorder point - discrete distribution solution				
Safety stock		Carrying cost	Stockout cost	Total cost
0		0	180	180
10		70	54	124
20		140	0	140
Original reorder point		70		
Best safety stock		10		
Revised reorder point		80		
Minimal cost		124		

Because the original reorder point is 50 and the lead time demands vary from 70 to 110, a maximum of (90-70) 20 units as safety stock is needed, so the results are given for values between 0 and 20 units. In each of these three cases, the carrying costs, stockout costs, and total costs are computed and displayed. Below the computations are the summary results.

Job Shop Scheduling (Sequencing)

The job shop scheduling models are used to solve one- and two-machine job shop problems. For the one-machine problem, the available methods are shortest processing time, first come first served, due date scheduling, Moore's method, slack time, slack per operation, longest processing time, and critical ratio. For two-machine scheduling, Johnson's method is used to minimize the makespan.

One-Machine Scheduling

Suppose that six employees are to be trained to operate different machines by a single trainer who can train only one person at a time. The time to train each person varies and is given in the accompanying table along with due dates and the number of operations involved.

Job	Time	Due Date	Number of Operations
Janet	3 days	4	2
Barry	5	7	4
Alexis	4	13	1
Sammy	7	10	2
Lisa	9	15	1
Ernie	2	5	3

Both the data and a solution appear in the next screen. We explain the data first.

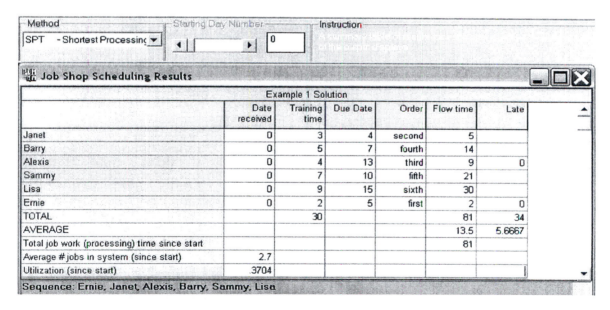

Methods (priority rules). The rules available for scheduling include:

1. Shortest processing time (SPT)
2. First come first serve (FCFS)
3. Earliest due date (Due Date)
4. Slack time (Slack)
5. Slack per operation (Slack/op)
6. Moore's method (Moore)
7. Longest processing time (LPT)
8. Critical ratio (Crit rat)

The data to be entered are as follows:

Starting day number. An optional starting day number may be given. Example 2 displays the use of this option.

Date received. It is possible to list the date each job is received. This information will be used in scheduling when first come first served is used. If receipt dates are given, they will be used in the computation of the flow times (see Example 2). The receipt days must be less than or equal to the starting day. That is, all jobs must be received on or before the starting date.

Job names. Names can be entered for each job.

Machine name. "Machine 1" at the top of the column can be changed to give the name of the type of machine. In this example, the process has been renamed "Training."

Processing time. The amount of time that each job will take on each machine is entered in the column labeled with the machine name.

Due date. In some instances, due dates are used. These are entered here.

Number of operations. In order to use the slack per operation rule, it is necessary to give a positive number of operations. All other methods ignore this column.

Example 1: Shortest processing time

The results depend on the rule that is chosen. In the first example, shortest processing time is used, but in going through the examples, all of the information that will be displayed is explained. The output for the first example is shown in the preceding screen.

Job order. A column is displayed that shows when each person (job) will be trained (processed). In Example 1, the column shows that Janet will be second, Barry fourth, Alexis third, Sammy fifth, Lisa sixth, and Ernie will be first.

Sequence. The same sequence is displayed but in a different manner at the bottom of the screen. In this example, the sequence is Ernie followed by Janet, Alexis, Barry Sammy, and Lisa.

Flow time. The time at which each job ends is given in a column of flow times. In the example, Ernie is the first one trained and ends after the processing time of 2 days. Janet is the second trained and ends after 3 more days at time 5. The last job performed, Lisa, ends after 30 days.

Completion time. If the starting day is not 0, a column of completion times is given that includes the starting day (see Example 2).

Tardiness or lateness. If due dates are given, the difference between the flow time and the due date is displayed. (On the screen the display is in red.) This difference will never be below 0. There is generally no such thing as early in scheduling. Late days are displayed in red on the screen.

Totals. For both the flow time and the lateness, the totals are computed and displayed.

Averages. More relevant than the totals are the averages. The average flow time represents the speed with which jobs leave the system after they have entered. The average lateness (tardiness) represents how badly the schedule is performing with respect to the promised due dates.

NOTE: The average lateness is computed based on all jobs, not only the jobs that are late. In the example, it is 34/6, even though Ernie and Alexis were trained on time.

Total job work (processing) time since start. If the starting times are 0, then this is simply the total flow time as in this example. Example 2 will display a different situation.

Average number of jobs in the system. This is computed as the total flow time (81) divided by the maximum flow time (30).

Utilization. This is computed as the maximum flow time (30) divided by the total flow time (81).

Gantt Chart

A Gantt chart illustrating the scheduling on the machine is available, as seen in the following screen:

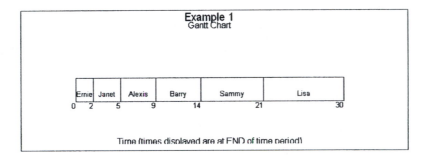

Example 1
Gantt Chart

| Ernie | Janet | Alexis | Barry | Sammy | Lisa |

0   2   5   9   14   21   30

Time (times displayed are at END of time period)

Summary

One of the output windows for one machine scheduling is a summary of results for all methods displayed as follows.

Method summary

Example 1 Solution							
Method	Sequence	Average flow time	Utilization	Ave # in system	Number late	Ave lateness
SPT - Shortest Processing Time	Ernie, Janet, Alexis,	13.5	.3704	2.7	4	5.6667
FCFS - First Come First Serve	Janet, Barry, Alexis,	16.6667	.3	3.3333	4	8
Slack - Due date minus processing time	Janet, Barry, Sammy,	16.5	.303	3.3	5	7.6667
EDD - Earliest Due Date	Janet, Ernie, Barry,	14.3333	.3488	2.8667	4	5.5
Moore - Minimize the number of late jobs	Janet, Ernie, Alexis,	13.6667	.3659	2.7333	3	5.5
LPT - Longest processing time	Lisa, Sammy, Barry,	21.5	.2326	4.3	5	13.5
Crit rat - (due date-today)/processing time	Janet, Barry, Sammy,	17.6667	.283	3.5333	5	8.8333

Example 2: First come first served

In the following example, the rule is first come first served and in addition receipt days for the jobs and a starting day of 100 have been added.

Method	Starting Day Number	Instruction
FCFS - First Come First Se ▼	◄ [ ] ►	100	This cell can not be changed.

Example 2				
	Date received	Production time	Due Date	# Opns
Janet	98	3	104	2
Barry	87	5	107	4
Alexis	99	4	113	1
Sammy	93	7	110	2
Lisa	82	9	115	1
Ernie	95	2	105	3

The results follow.

Job Shop Scheduling Results							
Example 2 Solution							
	Date received	Production time	Due Date	Order	Flow time	Completion time	Late
Janet	98	3	104	fifth	28	125	21
Barry	87	5	107	second	27	113	6
Alexis	99	4	113	sixth	31	129	16
Sammy	93	7	110	third	28	120	10
Lisa	82	9	115	first	27	108	0
Ernie	95	2	105	fourth	28	122	17
TOTAL		30			169	717	70
AVERAGE					28.1667	119.5	11.6667
Total job work (processing) time since start					123		
Average # jobs in system (since start)	4.1						
Utilization (since start)	.2439						

Sequence: Lisa, Barry, Sammy, Ernie, Janet, Alexis

Because the first come first served (FCFS) option is selected, the program will schedule the jobs according to the receipt day.

Notice that there is an extra column of results named "Completion time." This is the flow time plus the starting day minus 1. For example, Lisa's job began at the beginning of day 100, was worked on for 9 days and therefore was finished at the end of day 108. Completion times are at the **end** of that day.

Now notice that the first job done, Lisa's job, was in the system from day 82 until its completion time at day 108. This is a flow time of 108 - 82 + 1 or 27 even though the scheduling does not begin until day 100. However, Lisa's job was in the system for only 9 days since day 100 (the start of the problem). The value 9 is what is used for computing the total job work processing time of 123, which is less than the total flow time of 169. The difference is that the total flow time *includes* the waiting that occurred before day 100 whereas the total processing time of 123 does not include any waiting before the start of the problem. The average number of jobs in the system and the utilization begin at the start day of 100.

Example 3: Schedule according to slack

Slack is defined as the due date minus the time required to process a job. In order to use slack, the due date must be given.

	Date received	oduction time	Due Date	Slack	Order	Flow time	Completion time	Late
Janet	1	3	4	1	first	3	3	0
Barry	1	5	7	2	second	8	8	1
Alexis	1	4	13	9	sixth	30	30	17
Sammy	1	7	10	3	third	15	15	5
Lisa	1	9	15	6	fifth	26	26	11
Ernie	1	2	5	3	fourth	17	17	12
TOTAL		30				99	99	46
AVERAGE						16.5	16.5	7.6667
Total job work (processing) time since						99		
Average # jobs in system (since start)	3.3							
Utilization (since start)	.303							

Sequence: Janet, Barry, Sammy, Ernie, Lisa, Alexis

The slack column did not appear before but does now. It is the difference between the due column and the "training" column. For example, Janet must be trained by day 4 but it takes 3 days to train, so there is 1 day of slack. The jobs are scheduled according to increasing order of slack. Janet has the least and is scheduled first, whereas Alexis has the most (9) and is scheduled last. The solution appears in the preceding screen.

Example 4: Slack time per operation

The data in the number of operations column has been used. The output (not shown) contains a new column titled slack/op, which is generated by dividing the slack by the number of operations. For example, the 1 day of slack for job 1 is divided by the 2 operations, yielding a slack per operation value of .5. Jobs are scheduled according to increasing order of slack per operation. Therefore, Janet is first (.5) and Alexis is last (9). (Ties are broken arbitrarily.)

Example 5: Due date scheduling

Janet is the first one due and is scheduled first, whereas Lisa is the last one due and is scheduled last.

Example 6: Moore's method

Moore's method minimizes the number of late jobs. In the example shown next, Moore's method leads to the sequence Janet, Ernie, Alexis, Barry, Sammy, Lisa which has three jobs late. No schedule will have fewer than three jobs late as can be seen in the summary table displayed at the end of Example 1.

Job Shop Scheduling Results

Example 6 Solution

	Date received	Production time	Due Date	Order	Flow time	Completion time	Late
Janet	1	3	4	first	3	3	0
Barry	1	5	7	fourth	14	14	7
Alexis	1	4	13	third	9	9	0
Sammy	1	7	10	fifth	21	21	11
Lisa	1	9	15	sixth	30	30	15
Ernie	1	2	5	second	5	5	0
TOTAL		30			82	82	33
AVERAGE					13.6667	13.6667	5.5
Total job work (processing) time since					82		
Average # jobs in system (since start)	2.7333						
Utilization (since start)	.3659						

Sequence: Janet, Ernie, Alexis, Barry, Sammy, Lisa

Example 7: Longest processing time

The LPT method schedules jobs from longest to shortest. This is typically the worst way to perform scheduling. In the example (not shown), LPT yields the sequence Lisa, Sammy, Barry, Alexis, Janet, Ernie, which is exactly opposite the SPT schedule of course. This schedule has an average flow time of 21.5 days. No schedule will have a larger average flow time. This schedule has 4.3 jobs in the system on average. No schedule will have a larger average number of jobs in the system.

Example 8: Critical ratio

The critical ratio is defined as (due date - today)/processing time. This is the first example in which the starting day number above the data has been used to compute the job priority. Jobs are scheduled in ascending order of the critical ratio. In this example, the schedule is Janet, Barry, Sammy, Ernie, Lisa, Alexis. Notice in the screen that there is an extra column of output, completion time. Because jobs do not start at time 0, the flow time and the completion time are different. For example, Janet is the first job done and begins today on day 3. Because it takes 3 days, Janet is worked on during days 3, 4, and 5, which becomes the completion time. The job is 1 day late.

Method	Starting Day Number	Instruction
Crit rat - (due date-today)/prc ▼	◄ [ ] ► 3	A summary table of results for each priority rule is available i of the output displays.

Job Shop Scheduling Results   _ □

Example 8 Solution								
	Date received	Production time	Due Date	Critical Ratio	Order	Flow time	Completion time	Late
Janet	3	3	4	.3333	first	3	5	1
Barry	3	5	7	.8	second	8	10	3
Alexis	3	4	13	2.5	sixth	30	32	19
Sammy	3	7	10	1	third	15	17	7
Lisa	3	9	15	1.3333	fifth	26	28	13
Ernie	3	2	5	1	fourth	17	19	14
TOTAL		30				99	111	57
AVERAGE						16.5	18.5	9.5
Total job work (processing) time since						99		
Average # jobs in system (since start)	3.3							
Utilization (since start)	.303							

Sequence: Janet, Barry, Sammy, Ernie, Lisa, Alexis

Two-Machine Scheduling

Consider the following problem. A typing center needs to type and print jobs for seven customers. The length of time that each job requires for final corrections (typing) and for printing is displayed in the following table. Each job must first have the typing finished before it can be duplicated.

Customer	Typing	Duplicating
Harry	20 minutes	19 minutes
Deb	43	27
Leah	37	38
Dara	62	11
Art	80	52
Sharon	12	36
Rivka	25	41

In the next screen, the two-machine problem is demonstrated. Johnson's method is used, and the order and sequence are listed as follows.

Job Shop Scheduling Results					
2-machine scheduling solution					
	Type	Duplicate	Order	Done 1	Done 2 (flow time)
Harry	20	19	seventh	253	286
Deb	43	27	sixth	233	267
Leah	37	38	third	74	127
Dara	62	11	eighth	315	326
Art	80	52	fourth	154	206
Sharon	12	36	first	12	48
Rivka	25	41	second	37	89
Gordon	36	34	fifth	190	240
Makespan					326

Sequence: Sharon, Rivka, Leah, Art, Gordon, Deb, Harry, Dara

In addition, the time at which each job ends on each machine is displayed. The largest of all of these times is the makespan, or time at which all work is completed; it is displayed at the bottom. In this example, it will take 326 minutes to finish the work.

Johnson's Method Steps

A secondary output for this submodel is the display of the order in which jobs were chosen according to Johnson's method. This is displayed in the following screen.

Johnson's Method Steps		
2-machine scheduling solution		
Step	Job	Position
1	Dara	8
2	Sharon	1
3	Harry	7
4	Rivka	2
5	Deb	6
6	Gordon	5
7	Leah	3
8	Art	4

The smallest time among the 14 times was 11 minutes for Dara on duplicating. Thus, Dara is scheduled last because duplicating is the second machine. The next smallest time among all customers except Dara is 12 for Sharon on typing. Because typing is the first process, Sharon is scheduled first. The method continues to find the smallest time of all unscheduled customers and schedules the customer as soon as possible if the time is on typing and as late as possible if the time is on duplicating.

A two-machine Gantt chart can be displayed as follows. If the name of the job is too long for the bar in the chart, then it will be truncated. For example, see Sharon on machine 1.

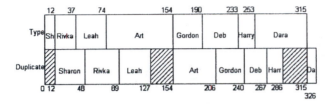

2-machine scheduling
Gantt Chart

 **Layout**

The facility layout model is used to place departments in rooms in order to minimize the total distance traveled as a function of the distances among the rooms and the flow among departments. In some cases, it is necessary to fix certain departments to be located in specific rooms. Distances among rooms may or may not be symmetric. (Usually they are, but this is not required.)

Data

The framework for layout is given by the number of departments or the number of rooms that we assume to be the same, since each department must be assigned to one and only one room.

The data that follows essentially consists of *two* tables of numbers, one for the flows and one for the distances.

Distances	Method	Instruction
⊙ Symmetric ○ Not Symmetric	Explicit enumeration ▼	Enter the flow from materials to Materials. Any real value is permissible.

Chapter 9: Problem 9.2							
Flow Table	Materials	Welding	Drills	Lathes	Grinders	Benders	Fixed room
Materials	0	100	50	0	0	50	
Welding	25	0	0	50	0	0	
Drills	25	0	0	0	50	0	
Lathes	0	25	0	0	20	0	
Grinders	50	0	100	0	0	0	
Benders	10	0	20	0	0	0	

Distance Table	Room 1	Room 2	Room 3	Room 4	Room 5	Room 6	
Room 1	0	20	40	20	40	60	
Room 2	20	0	20	40	20	40	
Room 3	40	20	0	60	40	20	
Room 4	20	40	60	0	20	40	
Room 5	40	20	40	20	0	20	
Room 6	60	40	20	40	20	0	

Method. There are two methods available. The default method is explicit enumeration. This is guaranteed to find the optimal solution. Unfortunately, if the problem size is too large, this method will take too much time. A second method, pairwise comparison is available. Unfortunately, this method is not guaranteed to always find the best layout.

Interdepartmental flows. The number of trips from one department to another is indicated in a table termed the *flow matrix.*

Distance matrix. The distance between rooms is entered in this table. Typically, the distance matrix will be symmetric. The choice is made at the beginning of the module. That is, the distance from Room *i* to Room *j* is the same distance as from Room *j* to Room *i*.

A sample set of data appears in the preceding screen. Notice in this example that the distances are symmetric.

Solution

The solution simply is to assign the departments to the appropriate rooms. The total movement is also noted.

Layout Results	
Room assignments	
Department	Room
Total Movement	13,000
Materials	Room 2
Welding	Room 1
Drills	Room 6
Lathes	Room 4
Grinders	Room 5
Benders	Room 3

Room assignments. On the right of each department row will appear the room in which the department should be placed. In our example materials should be placed in Room 2, welding in Room 1, and so on.

Total movement. The sum of the products of the number of trips multiplied by the distance is listed at the top. This is what should be minimized. Notice that for the example the minimum total movement is 13,000.

It is possible to display the individual multiplications of room-to-room distances by process-to-process flows. This is shown (partially) in the screen that follows.

Dept. to dept. flow table

From Department	Room	To Department	Room	Distance	Trips	Total (Trips*Distance)
		Chapter 9: Problem 9.2 Solution				
Materials	Room 2	Materials	Room 2	0	0	0
		Welding	Room 1	20	100	2,000
		Drills	Room 6	40	50	2,000
		Lathes	Room 4	40	0	0
		Grinders	Room 5	20	0	0
		Benders	Room 3	20	50	1,000
Welding	Room 1	Materials	Room 2	20	25	500
		Welding	Room 1	0	0	0
		Drills	Room 6	60	0	0
		Lathes	Room 4	20	50	1,000
		Grinders	Room 5	40	0	0
		Benders	Room 3	40	0	0
Drills	Room 6	Materials	Room 2	40	25	1,000
		Welding	Room 1	60	0	0
		Drills	Room 6	0	0	0
		Lathes	Room 4	40	0	0
		Grinders	Room 5	20	50	1,000
		Benders	Room 3	20	0	0
Lathes	Room 4	Materials	Room 2	40	0	5

In order to demonstrate pairwise comparison, we take the same example but change the method and solve it. The results are displayed below. Notice that, indeed, pairwise comparison did not find the optimal solution since the movement under pairwise comparison, 15,200, is larger than the movement under explicit enumeration.

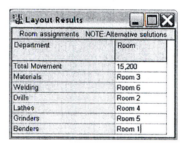

Layout Results

Room assignments NOTE:Alternative solutions

Department	Room
Total Movement	15,200
Materials	Room 3
Welding	Room 6
Drills	Room 2
Lathes	Room 4
Grinders	Room 5
Benders	Room 1

Fixing Departments in Specific Rooms

If the room name appears in the column labeled "Fixed Room," that department will be fixed in that room. Suppose that in the previous example materials must be placed in Room 1. Then, to accomplish this, "room 1" is placed in the row for materials in the "Fixed Room" column using the drop-down box.

Flow Table	Materials	Welding	Drills	Lathes	Grinders	Benders	Fixed room
			Chapter 9: Problem 9.2				
Materials	0	100	50	0	0	50	Room 1 ▼
Welding	25	0	0	50	0	0	<none>
Drills	25	0	0	0	50	0	Room 1
Lathes	0	25	0	0	20	0	Room 2
Grinders	50	0	100	0	0	0	Room 3
Benders	10	0	20	0	0	0	Room 4
							Room 5
Distance Table	Room 1	Room 2	Room 3	Room 4	Room 5	Room 6	Room 6
Room 1	0	20	40	20	40	60	
Room 2	20	0	20	40	20	40	
Room 3	40	20	0	60	40	20	
Room 4	20	40	60	0	20	40	
Room 5	40	20	40	20	0	20	
Room 6	60	40	20	40	20	0	

The solution follows. The room assignments are, of course, different, and the total movement is, of course, greater than before.

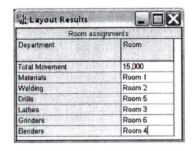

Layout Results	
Room assignments	
Department	Room
Total Movement	15,000
Materials	Room 1
Welding	Room 2
Drills	Room 5
Lathes	Room 3
Grinders	Room 6
Benders	Room 4

Learning (Experience) Curves

Two models are available for learning curves. In the first model, it is assumed that the learning coefficient is known; in the second model, it is assumed that the production time for 2 units is known and that the learning curve coefficient is computed based on these. In either case, the production times for units from 1 to a specified number and the cumulative production time for these units can be found. In addition, for either model the learning curve can be graphed.

The Data

Consider a situation in which unit 1 took 10 hours, the learning curve coefficient is 90 percent, and the interest is in the first 20 units. Following is a screen that contains both the data and the one line of primary output:

Parameter	Value
Learning Curves Results	
Example 1 Solution	
Display times given a learning coefficient	
Unit number of base unit	1
Labor time for base unit,Y1	10
Unit number of last unit,N	20
Learning coefficient	.9
Time for last unit	6.3422

Unit number of base unit. This is usually 1 as in the example, but it can be set to any number.

Time for base unit. This is the length of time that it takes to manufacture the unit number as specified above. In the example, it is 10 hours.

Number of the last unit. This is the item number for the last unit that will be displayed or used for computations. In the example, we are interested in unit 20 or the first 20 units.

Learning curve coefficient. This is a number between 0 and 1. It is the percentage of the first unit's time that it takes to make the second unit and also the percentage of the second unit's time that it takes to make the *fourth* unit. The learning curve coefficient is only entered for the first model. The second model will determine the learning curve coefficient based on the next data input item.

Time to make last unit. Not shown on this screen, but shown in the next example, the last piece of information for the second model is the time it takes to produce the last unit rather than the learning curve coefficient. Based on this piece of information, the learning curve coefficient will be determined (see Example 2).

Example 1: Computing times and cumulative times

The sample problem appears in the preceding screen. The four lines of input data indicate that the first unit (Unit 1) takes 10 minutes to manufacture, the last unit is Unit 20, and the learning coefficient is 90 percent. That is, the decrease in time is such that, with the doubling of the unit number, the time is 90 percent of the previous time.

The solution in the preceding screen is that the last unit (20) takes 6.34 minutes.

An additional table of times and cumulative times can be displayed. The output consists of three columns.

Unit	Production Time	Cumulative Time
1	10	10
2	9	19
3	8.4621	27.4621
4	8.1	35.5621
5	7.8299	43.3919
6	7.6159	51.0078
7	7.4395	58.4473
8	7.29	65.7373
9	7.1606	72.8979
10	7.0469	79.9448
11	6.9455	86.8903
12	6.8543	93.7446
13	6.7714	100.516
14	6.6955	107.2115
15	6.6257	113.8372
16	6.561	120.3982
17	6.5008	126.899
18	6.4445	133.3436
19	6.3918	139.7354

Unit number. This runs from 1 to the last unit, which in our example is 20. The two additional columns are as follows:

Time to produce a single unit (production time). This column contains the time to produce a unit. For example, it takes 10 minutes to produce Unit 1 (as specified by the input), 9 minutes to produce Unit 2 (as computed using the learning coefficient), 8.1 minutes to produce Unit 4 (90 percent of 9 minutes), 7.29 minutes to produce Unit 8, and so on. The interesting numbers are the ones that are not powers of 2. For example, it takes 6.34 units to produce Unit 20.

Cumulative time. The last column contains the amount of time to produce all of the units up to and including that unit number. Obviously, it takes 10 minutes to produce Unit 1. It takes 19 minutes to produce Units 1 and 2; 35.20 minutes to produce the first four units; and 146.08 minutes to produce the first 20 units. A graph of the unit production times can be displayed. The scrollbar can be used to see the effects of the learning coefficient on the graph.

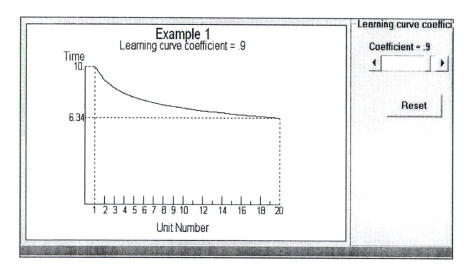

Example 2: Finding the learning curve coefficient

Following is the solution screen for an example of the second model. In this case, we know that Unit 4 took 73 minutes and Unit 37 took 68 minutes. The program has computed that, based on these two times, the learning curve coefficient is .9781.

Learning Curves Results	
Example 2: Finding the learning curve coefficient solution	
Parameter	Value
Find learning coefficient given 2 times	
Unit number of base unit	4
Labor time for base unit,Y1	73
Unit number of last unit,N	37
Labor time for last unit,YN	68
Learning curve coefficient	.9781

 Linear Programming

Any linear program is defined by the number of variables and the number of constraints. Do not count the non-negativity restrictions as constraints. Most linear programming packages (but not Excel's Solver) assume that unless told otherwise the variables must be non-negative.

Consider the following example with two constraints and two variables:

$$\text{maximize} \quad 3x + 3y$$
$$\text{subject to} \quad 3x + 4y \le 14 \text{ (labor hours)}$$
$$6x + 4y \le 15 \text{ (pounds of material)}$$
$$x, y \ge 0$$

The data screen for this appears next. The entire screen is displayed so that a STEP tool that now appears on the toolbar before the SOLVE tool can be seen. Also, **Step** is enabled in the **File** menu.

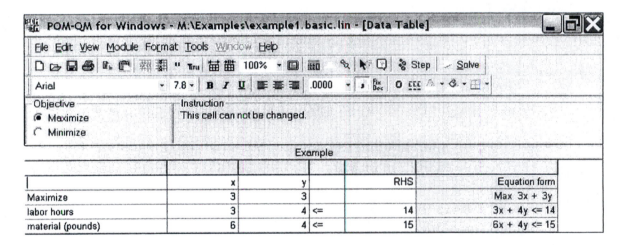

Objective function. The choice of minimization or maximization is made in the usual way at the time of problem creation, but it can be changed on the data screen using the objective option above the data.

Objective function coefficients. The cost/profit coefficients (typically referred to as c_j) are entered as numerical values. These coefficients may be positive or negative.

Constraint coefficients. The main body of information contains the constraint coefficients, which typically are called the $a_{ij}s$. These may be positive or negative.

Right-hand side (RHS) coefficients. The values on the right-hand side of the constraints are entered here. These are also termed the b_is. These must be non-negative.

The constraint sign. This can be entered in one of two ways. It is permissible to press the [<] key, the [>] key, or the [=] key. Alternatively, when you go to a cell with the constraint sign, a drop-down arrow appears in the cell, as shown in the following screen in Constraint 2 in the column with the constraint signs.

	x	y		RHS	Equation form
					Example
Maximize	3	3			Max 3x + 3y
labor hours	3	4	<=	14	3x + 4y <= 14
material (pounds)	6	4	<= ▼	15	6x + 4y <= 15

You can click on the arrow, bringing in a drop-down box as shown next:

	x	y		RHS	Equation form
					Example
Maximize	3	3			Max 3x + 3y
labor hours	3	4	<=	14	3x + 4y <= 14
material (pounds)	6	4	<= ▼	15	6x + 4y <= 15
			<=		
			=		
			>=		

Equation form. The column on the far right displays the equation form of the constraint and cannot be directly edited but changes as the coefficients, column name, sign, or right-hand side change.

The Solution

Following is the solution to the example. Please note that the display varies somewhat according to the textbook option selected in **Help, User Information.**

Linear Programming Results ⊟□✕

Example Solution	x	y			RHS	Dual
Maximize	3	3				
labor hours	3	4	<=		14	.5
material (pounds)	6	4	<=		15	.25
Solution->	.3333	3.25			10.75	

Optimal values for the variables. Underneath each column, the optimal values for the variables are given. In this example, *x* should be .33 and *y* should be 3.25.

Optimal cost/profit. In the lower right-hand corner of the table, the maximum profit or the minimum cost is given. In this example, the maximum profit is $10.75.

Shadow prices. The shadow (or dual) prices appear on the right of each constraint. In this example, we would pay .5 more for one more unit of resource 1 and .25 more for one more unit of resource 2.

The graph

One of the other output displays is a graph as shown in the following screen. The feasible region is shaded. On the right is a table of all of the feasible corner points and the value of the objective function (Z) at those points. In addition, the constraints and objective function can be highlighted in red by clicking on the option buttons on the right under "Constraint Display."

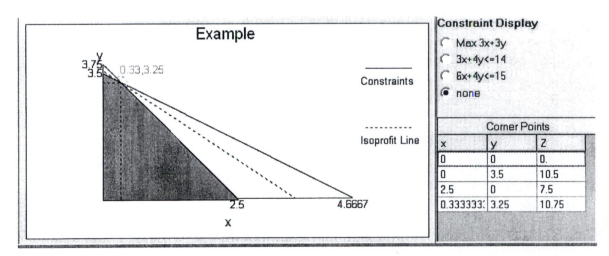

Table of Ranges

In addition to listing the values, additional information about the variables is provided. The interpretation of the additional information is left for your textbook. In the example, you can see the reduced cost, original objective value coefficient, and the lower and upper limits (the range) over which the solution will be the same. That is, the variables will take on the same values of .333 and 3.25; only the objective function value (profit or cost) will change.

NOTE: Some texts and other programs give the allowable decrease and increase (from the original value) rather than the upper and lower limits on the ranges.

◈ Ranging ▭▢✕

		Example Solution			
Variable	Value	Reduced Cost	Original Val	Lower Bound	Upper Bound
x	.3333	0	3	2.25	4.5
y	3.25	0	3	2	4
Constraint	Dual Value	Slack/Surplus	Original Val	Lower Bound	Upper Bound
labor hours	.5	0	14	7.5	15
material (pounds)	.25	0	15	14	28

Iterations

The iterations can also be displayed. The tableau style varies according to the textbook selected.

▦ Iterations ▭▢✕

Cj	Basic Variables	3 x	3 y	0 slack 1	0 slack 2	Quantity
Iteration 1						
	cj-zj	3	3	0	0	
0	slack 1	3	4	1	0	14
0	slack 2	6	4	0	1	15
Iteration 2						
	cj-zj	0	1	0	-0.5	
0	slack 1	0	2	1	-0.5	6.5
3	x	1	0.6667	0	0.1667	2.5
Iteration 3						
	cj-zj	0	0	-0.5	-0.25	
3	y	0	1	0.5	-0.25	3.25
3	x	1	0	-0.3333	0.3333	0.3333

Solution list

It is also possible to display the solution in a list, as shown next:

Solution list		
Example Solution		
Variable	Status	Value
x	Basic	.3333
y	Basic	3.25
slack 1	NONBasic	0
slack 2	NONBasic	0
Optimal Value (Z)		10.75

The dual problem

Another window of results displays the dual problem.

Dual				
Example Solution				
Original Problem				
Maximize	x	y		
labor hours	3	4	<=	14
material (pounds)	6	4	<=	15
Dual Problem				
	labor	material		
Minimize	14	15		
x	3	6	>=	3
y	4	4	>=	3

Stepping

If you look at the first screen at the beginning of this section on linear programming, you will notice that to the left of the SOLVE tool a STEP tool appears.

Although the iterations are available in the iteration output screen, it also is possible to step through and see the iterations one at a time. The major advantage of stepping is that *you* can select the entering variable. Press STEP and the screen appears as follows. (The display varies according to the textbook set in **Help, User Information**.)

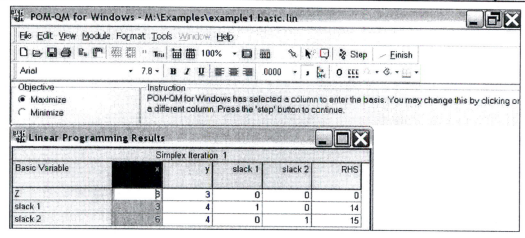

The software has created a simplex tableau adding two slack variables. The first column is highlighted because it has the highest profit contribution. If you want this column, press the STEP tool. If you want to change the pivot column, simply click on a different column and then press STEP. After one iteration the screen follows.

Basic Variable	x	y	slack 1	slack 2	RHS
Z	0	1	0	-.5	-7.5
slack 1	0	2	1	-.5	6.5
x	1	.6667	0	.1667	2.5

When the optimal solution is found, a message to that effect will appear in the instruction bar as follows. Because the software allows you to iterate *even after finding the optimal solution*, when you are done you must press the FINISH tool.

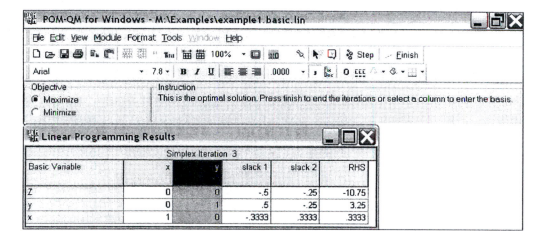

 **Location**

There are four facility location models. The first module is the standard qualitative/subjective weighting system. Several factors are identified that are considered to be important for the location decision. Weights are assigned to these factors, and scores for these factors are determined for the various possible sites. The program computes the weighted sum of the scores (and identifies the site with the *highest* score).

The second and third methods are quantitative methods for location on a line (one dimensional) or a plane (two dimensional). In the one-dimensional case, the coordinate or street number must be given; in the two-dimensional case, both a horizontal coordinate and a vertical coordinate must be given. In either case, the program will have a default weight of 1 trip per location, but this may be changed to reflect different numbers of trips or different weights of materials. The program will find the median location, the mean location, and total weighted and unweighted distances from each location.

NOTE: Some of the location models called one- and two-dimensional location are also known as "center of gravity" models in some textbooks

The last model is simply breakeven analysis applied to location problems.

The Qualitative (Weighting) Model

If the qualitative model is chosen, the general framework is given by the number of factors and the number of potential sites. The following screen shows an example with seven factors and three potential sites.

Factor weights. Weights should be given for each factor. The weights can be given as whole numbers or fractions. Generally, weights sum to 1 or 100, but this is *not* a requirement.

Scores. The score of each city on each factor should be given.

Example 1: Weighted location (qualitative) analysis

In the following screen, a filled-in sample, along with the solution is displayed. Notice that the cities and the factors have been named.

Location Results

Example 1 - Qualitative Analysis Solution				
	Weight	Philadelphia	Memphis	Springfield (IL)
labor supply	10	90	80	50
labor wages	30	80	60	70
transportation	5	60	70	50
banking	15	90	95	90
computer services	20	50	60	80
government	10	40	20	5
unemployment	5	30	50	70
Total	95			
Weighted Total		6,500	6,025	6,200
Weighted Average		68.4211	63.4211	65.2632

The output is very straightforward and consists of the following:

Total weighted score. For each city, the weights are multiplied by the scores for each factor and summed. The total is printed at the bottom of each column. For example, the score for Philadelphia has been computed as:

$$(10*90) + (30*80) + (5*60) + (15*90) + (20*50) + (10*40) + (5*30) = 6500$$

which appears at the bottom of the Philadelphia column.

The weighted average (total score/total weight) is also displayed for each location.

Example 2: One dimensional siting

If one-dimensional siting is chosen, the general framework consists of a column of weights or trips and a single coordinate or address column. The required information in order to get started is the number of sites to be included in the analysis.

The solution screen, which includes the data for a four-site analysis, is given in the following screen.

The information to be filled in is as follows:

Weight/trips. Include the weight or number of trips to or from each site. The default value is 1 for each location. This is what should be used when all customers (locations) are considered to be equal. If more trips are made to one customer than another, this can be included in the weight/trip column. If the number of trips is the same but the weight of the materials differs, this should be included.

Location Results			
Example 2: One-Dimensional Siting Solution			
	Weight/trips	x coord	Multiplication
site 1	6	1,100	6,600
site 2	2	2,800	5,600
site 3	1	3,300	3,300
site 4	4	6,500	26,000
Total	13	13,700	41,500
Unweighted Mean		3,425	
Weighted Mean			3,192.308
Median Trip	7	2,800	

x *coordinate*. The coordinate of the locations must be given. This can be expressed in several different ways. These may be street addresses (on the same street because this is one dimens;onal), they may be floors in a building (it is possible for the dimension to go up instead of across); or they may be east-west or north-south coordinates, where a negative number means west or south and a positive number means east or north.

Our sample problem with a solution appears in the previous screen. The output again is very straightforward.

Total weight or number of trips. In order to find the mean or median location, it is necessary to determine the total number of trips or total weight. In the example, there are 13 total trips so the middle trip is the seventh.

The mean location. This is the location that minimizes the sum of the squares of the distances of the trips.

The median trip. The median trip is identified as Trip 7 and occurs from the location at 2,800.

In general, an interesting question is whether a manager should minimize total distance or total distance squared. Notice in this example that one yields an answer at block 2,800 and the other yields an answer at block 3,100 to 3,200 (3192.308).

Two-Dimensional Siting

The information for two-dimensional siting is analogous to the information required for one-dimensional siting. Again, the only setup information is the number of locations. The following screen contains the data and solution for a two-dimensional siting problem. The only difference between the data for one- and two-dimensional sitings is the extra column that now appears for the second coordinate data. Data is to be entered in the same way as for a one-dimensional siting.

Location Results

Example 3: Two dimensional location/center of gravity solution					
	Weight/trips	EW coord	NS coord	X multiplied	Y multiplied
raw material 1	70	132	123	9,240	8,610
raw material 2	40	226	622	9,040	24,880
raw material 3	50	140	41	7,000	2,050
customer 1	90	99	75	8,910	6,750
customer 2	70	321	33	22,470	2,310
potential site 1	0	138	82	0	0
potential site 2	0	185	40	0	0
Total	320	1,241	1,016	56,660	44,600
Average		177.2857	145.1429		
Weighted Average				177.0625	139.375
Median	160			132	75

Example 3: Two-dimensional location

The solution screen for a two-dimensional siting has a large amount of information as exhibited in the preceding screen. Some of the information is the same as that of the one- dimensional siting and some is extra.

Weighted x-coordinate This is simply the coordinate multiplied by the number of trips. In the example, the number of trips is positive for each of the first five locations but 0 for the last two. The multiplications by the weights can be seen.

Weighted y-coordinate. This is identical to the previous column except that it is the *y* coordinate that is multiplied. These weighted columns demonstrate the computations that lead to the answers below the data. The average of these columns are the answers. Notice in this example that dividing by 7 yields the first (unweighted) average and dividing by the sum of the weights, which is 320, yields the second (weighted) average.

Median. The median trip is 160 (there is no 160.5), and the median *x* coordinate is 132, whereas the median *y* coordinate is 75.

Averages. The unweighted and weighted averages of the coordinates are displayed.

Table of distances

Tables of distances from point to point can be displayed.

Distance Table (Air/Straight line)									
Example 3: Two dimensional location/center of gravity solution									
	Center	Weighted Center	raw material 1	raw material 2	raw material 3	customer 1	customer 2	potential site 1	potential site 2
raw material 1	50.4094	47.9455	0	507.7765	82.3893	58.2495	209.3347	41.4367	98.4784
raw material 2	479.3389	485.0998	507.7765	0	587.3304	561.5496	596.6121	547.1234	583.4424
raw material 3	110.6163	105.125	82.3893	587.3304	0	53.2635	181.1767	41.0488	45.0111
customer 1	105.1127	101.1825	58.2495	561.5496	53.2635	0	225.938	39.6232	92.8493
customer 2	182.2905	178.9794	209.3347	596.6121	181.1767	225.938	0	189.4466	136.18
potential site 1	74.3666	69.4102	41.4367	547.1234	41.0488	39.6232	189.4466	0	63.0317
potential site 2	105.4255	99.6915	98.4784	583.4424	45.0111	92.8493	136.18	63.0317	0
Total	1,107.56	1,087.434	997.665	3,383.834	990.2198	1,031.473	1,538.688	921.7104	1,018.993
Weighted total	50,453.5	49,651.41	44,326.41	157,213.2	46,736.55	45,018.29	67,911.17	43,665.29	50,370.78

Total distance. For each column, the row named "Total" contains the total distance from every site to the site in that column. The means for computing the distance depends on the table (air distance versus city block distance). The number 997.665 for Raw Material 1 means that the site of Raw Material 1 at coordinates 132, 123 has a total distance of 997.67 from each of the other six sites. That is, if you made one trip from each of the six sites to the site of Raw Material 1, it would cover a distance of 997.67. Another way to view this column is to say that Potential site 1 is more central than Potential site 2 because it has a distance of 921.71, which is smaller than the 1018.99 of Potential site 2.

Weighted total. The numbers in the distance row do not take into account that different numbers of trips are made between points or that different amounts of material are moved between points. This column multiplies the distance times the number of trips or amount of materials moved. Again, though, Potential site 1 seems to have the advantage over Potential site 2.

NOTE: It is possible, and maybe even useful, to solve the one-dimensional problem using the two-dimensional model with one coordinate equal to 0 for all sites.

Example 4: Breakeven analysis

One more model is available. This is simply a breakeven analysis model because breakeven can be applied to location problems. Following is an example. The crossover points are found and a graph is available.

Example 4: Locational Breakeven Analysis Solution	Location 1	Location 2	Location 3
Fixed costs	100000	140000	188000
Variable costs	15	14.3	13.9
BREAKEVEN POINTS	Units	Dollars	
Location 1 vs Location 2	57143	957145	
Location 1 vs Location 3	80000	1300000	
Location 2 vs Location 3	120000	1856000	
Volume analysis @	30000		
Total Fixed Costs	100000	140000	188000
Total Variable Costs/Revenues	450000	429000	417000
Total Costs	550000	569000	605000

 # Lot Sizing

The lot sizing model is used for determining total holding, setup, and stockout costs when demands are not equal in each period. Standard methods include the economic order quantity (EOQ); period order quantity (POQ); lot-for-lot; part-period balancing method; and Wagner-Whitin, which finds the optimal schedule. Lot sizing is almost invariably discussed in association with MRP systems.

The Data

Consider the following example:

Week	Demand
July 11	5
July 18	2
July 25	4
August 1	8
August 8	9
August 15	3

Holding costs are $2 per unit per week and the cost to set up a production run is $21. There is no initial inventory or lead time.

A data screen for the problem appears next. The data to be given includes demands on the left and costs and other information on the right of the table.

Method			Instruction		
Wagner - Whitin ▼			Enter the value for august 15 for value. Any non-negative value is permissible		

			Example	
Period	Demand		Parameter	Value
July 11	5		Holding Cost	2
July 18	2		Setup Cost	21
July 25	4		Stockout cost	0
August 1	8		Initial Inventory	0
August 8	9		Lead time	0
August 15	3			

Six methods are available in the method box above the data.

1. Wagner-Whitin finds the production schedule, which minimizes the total costs (holding + setup).

2. Lot-for-lot is the traditional MRP way of ordering exactly what is needed in every period. (This is optimal if setup costs are 0.)

3. The EOQ method computes the EOQ based on the average demand over the period and orders in lots of this size. Enough lots are ordered to cover the demand.

4. The period order quantity (POQ) translates the EOQ into time units (number of periods), rather than an order quantity. The POQ is the length of time an EOQ order will cover, rounded off to an integer. For example, if the demand rate averages 100 units per period and the EOQ is 20 units per order, the POQ is 100/20 = 5 periods.

5. Part-period balancing is a well-known, widely used heuristic that is covered in many books.

6. In the user-defined option, the user may define the production quantities.

Demands. The demands in each period are to be given. The demands are integers.

Produce. This column is used only for the user-defined option. Enter the number of units to be produced. If an option other than user-defined is chosen, the program will revise this column and display it as output.

The information on the right includes:

Holding cost. The cost of holding 1 unit for 1 period is to be entered here. The holding cost is charged against the inventory at the end of the period.

Shortage cost. The cost of being short 1 unit for 1 period is to be entered here. The shortage cost is charged against the inventory at the end of the period if the inventory is negative. Because of lead time or under the user-defined option, it is possible for the inventory to be negative. (For example, the user could define production to be 0 in every period).

NOTE: It is generally assumed that the holding and shortage costs are charged against the inventory that is on hand at the *end* of the period.

Setup cost. This is the cost of each production run. It is charged only in the periods that have positive production.

Initial inventory. It is possible to allow for a situation where there is beginning inventory.

Lead time. This will offset the requirements and produce *n* periods earlier. (See Example 3.)

Example 1: A six-period lot sizing problem

Period	Demand	Order receipt	Inventory	Holding Cost $2.00	Setup Cost $21.00
Initial Inventory			0		
July 11	5	11	6	12	21
July 18	2		4	8	
July 25	4		0		
August 1	8	8	0		21
August 8	9	12	3	6	21
August 15	3		0		
Totals	31	31	13	26	63
Average demand	5.17				
Total cost =	89				

The solution for the example is displayed in the preceding screen. The order receipt column has been derived by the program. The extra columns that are derived contain the following information:

Inventory. This is the amount of inventory on hand at the *end* of the period. In the example, there are 6 units left after Period 1, 4 units left after Period 2, and 3 units on hand after Period 5. The holding cost is charged against these amounts.

Holding cost. This is the cost of holding inventory at the end of a period. It is simply the number of units on hand multiplied by the holding cost per unit, which in this example is $2.

Setup cost. This is $0 if no production occurs, or the setup cost if production occurs during this period. In the example, setups occur in Periods 1, 4, and 5, so the setup cost of $21 is listed in these 3 periods but not in the other 3 periods.

Totals. The total inventory, holding costs, and setup costs are listed at the bottom of each column. Thirteen units were held for one month at a cost of $26.00. Three setups occurred at a total cost of $63.

Total cost. The sum of the setup and holding costs is displayed in the bottom left hand corner. The total cost in this example is $89. Because we used Wagner-Whitin, this solution is optimal.

Example 2: Using the EOQ

One of the options for placing orders is to use the economic order quantity. The EOQ is computed based on the average demand over the periods. In the example, the EOQ is based on the demand rate of 31 units per 6 periods (31/6 = 5.167). Using the holding cost and setup cost with this demand generates an EOQ of 10 (after rounding), as shown near the bottom of the following screen. The program will place an order for 10 units every time that the inventory is insufficient to cover the demand. For example, the first order for 10 units is placed in Period 1. This covers the demand in Period 1 and the demand in Period 2. In period 3, another order of 10 units is needed. Using this method in the example generates four orders (which total 40 units, not 31 units) and a total cost of $142.

Method: Economic Order Quantity

This may not be optimal. Use Wagner/Whitin for optimal lot sizes.

Lot Sizing Results

Example Solution

Period	Demand	Order receipt	Inventory	Holding Cost $2.00	Setup Cost $21.00
Initial Inventory			0		
July 11	5	10	5	10	21
July 18	2		3	6	
July 25	4	10	9	18	21
August 1	8		1	2	
August 8	9	10	2	4	21
August 15	3	10	9	18	21
Totals	31	40	29	58	84
Average demand	5.17	EOQ =	10		
Total cost =	142				

Note that the EOQ method will likely order more units than needed and, therefore, have higher holding costs than necessary.

Example 3: Using the POQ

The previous two examples have been modified by adding an initial inventory of 6 units and a lead time of 1 week. Also the method has been changed to the POQ.

One of the options for placing orders is to use the period order quantity. The POQ is the EOQ but expressed in time rather than units. In our example, the POQ is the 10 units divided by the average demand rate and rounded off, which is 2 periods, as seen in the following screen. The program will place an order to cover every 2 periods.

Method					
Period Order Quantity ▼	This may not be optimal. Use Wagner/Whitin for optimal lot sizes.				

Lot Sizing Results — ▢ ☐ ☒

Period	Demand	Order receipt	Inventory	Holding Cost $2.00	Setup Cost $21.00
Initial Inventory			0		
July 11	5	7	2	4	21
July 18	2		0		
July 25	4	12	8	16	21
August 1	8		0		
August 8	9	12	3	6	21
August 15	3		0		
Totals	31	31	13	26	63
Average demand	5.17	EOQ =	10		
Total cost =	89	POQ =	2		

Because there is lead time, the results screen includes an extra column for the order release. For example, the order due on July 18 must be released on July 11 as a result of this lead time. The order quantities are the same as without the lead time, but the orders are released earlier because of the lead time. Notice that if a 1 week lead time had been used but not added to the initial inventory to cover the first period, then there would have been an unavoidable shortage in Period 1.

Example 4: Lot-for-lot ordering

Lot-for-lot ordering (not shown) is a straightforward and common way for MRP systems to operate. The exact amount demanded is always ordered. This is optimal if there is no setup cost.

Markov Analysis

A Markov Chain is described by a transition matrix that gives the probability of going from state to state. For example, consider the following:

Example 1: A simple Markov chain

From/To	State 1	State 2	State 3
State 1	.7	.1	.2
State 2	.05	.85	.1
State 3	.05	.05	.9

From State 1, there is a 70 percent chance that State 1 will be the state at the next stage, a 10 percent chance State 2 will be the state at the next stage, and a 20 percent chance that State 3 will be the state at the next stage. There are essentially two types of questions that need to be answered for Markov Chains: (1) Where will be the state after a small number of steps? (2) what will be the state after a large number of steps? Often this depends on the state in which the chain begins.

The data screen for this example is shown next. The first column ("Initial") indicates that there is an equal chance of starting in any of the three states. This column does *not* have to contain probabilities as shown in Example 2. The number of transitions above the data table indicates that results after 3 transitions are to be examined.

Number of transitions		Instruction
◄	3	Enter the name for this state. Almost any character is permissible.

Example 1				
	Initial	State 1	State 2	State 3
State 1	.3333	.7	.1	.2
State 2	.3333	.05	.85	.1
State 3	.3333	.05	.05	.9

Results

The results screen contains three different types of answers. The top 3-by-3 table contains the three-step transition matrix (which is independent of the starting state). The next row gives the probability that we end in State 1 or 2 or 3, which *is* a function of the initial state probabilities. The last row gives the long-run probability (steady state probability) or the percentage of time spent in each state.

Markov Analysis Results ▬ ☐ ✕

Example 1 3 step transition matrix			
	State 1	State 2	State 3
State 1	.3783	.2073	.4145
State 2	.1036	.6401	.2563
State 3	.1036	.1281	.7682
Ending probability (given initial)	.1952	.3252	.4797
Steady State probability	.1429	.2857	.5714

The following screen displays the multiplications through three transitions (as requested in the extra data box above the data).

Multiplications ▬ ☐ ✕

Example 1 Solution			
	State 1	State 2	State 3
End of Period 1			
State 1	.7	.1	.2
State 2	.05	.85	.1
State 3	.05	.05	.9
End prob (given initial)	.2667	.3333	.4
End of Period 2			
State 1	.505	.165	.33
State 2	.0825	.7325	.185
State 3	.0825	.0925	.825
End prob (given initial)	.2233	.33	.4467
End of Period 3			
State 1	.3783	.2073	.4145
State 2	.1036	.6401	.2563
State 3	.1036	.1281	.7682

Example 2: A complete analysis

Consider the Markov Chain that is displayed next. The chain consists of three different types of states. State 1 is absorbing; states 3 and 4 together form a closed, recurrent class; state 2 is transient. Furthermore, at the beginning of this problem there are 60, 80,100, and 60 (total = 300) items in States 1, 2, 3, and 4 respectively. As previously stated, the initial column does not have to contain probabilities.

	Initial	State 1	State 2	State 3	State 4
			Example 2		
State 1	60	1	0	0	0
State 2	80	.2	.3	.4	.1
State 3	100	0	0	.5	.5
State 4	60	0	0	.5	.5

The first output table, as in the previous example, describes long-run behavior. The top of the table contains the long-run probabilities. The ending number row indicates the expected number (in the statistical sense) of how many of the original 300 items will end up in each state. In this example, the 60 that started in State 1 will end in state 1 and the 160 that started in States 3 and 4 will end in those states (divided evenly). Of the 80 that started in State 2, 28.57 percent (22.857) will end up in State 1, whereas the others will be split evenly over states 3 and 4.

Markov Analysis Results

	State 1	State 2	State 3	State 4
		Example 2 Steady state transition matrix		
State 1	1	0	0	0
State 2	.2857	0	.3571	.3571
State 3	0	0	.5	.5
State 4	0	0	.5	.5
Ending number (given initial)	82.8572	0	108.5714	108.5714
Steady State probability	1	0	.5	.5

The steady state probabilities in the bottom row all need to be interpreted as conditional on the closed recurrent class in which the states are. For example, first note that they do not sum to 1. These classes are identified in a second output screen, as follows:

State analysis

State	Type	Class number
	Example 2 Solution	
State 1	Absorbing	1
State 2	Transient	
State 3	Recurrent	2
State 4	Recurrent	2

Finally, there is one more output screen. This screen contains the usual Markov matrices that are generated when performing a Markov Chain analysis. The top matrix is a sorted version of the original Markov Chain. It is sorted so that all states in the same recurrent class are adjacent (see States 3 and 4) and so that the transient states are last (State 2).

Matrices				
Example 2 Solution				
Markov Matrix (sorted if	State 1	State 3	State 4	State 2
State 1	1	0	0	0
State 3	0	.5	.5	0
State 4	0	.5	.5	0
State 2	.2	.4	.1	.3
B matrix	State 2			
State 2	.3			
F matrix (I-B)^-1	State 2			
State 2	1.4286			
FA matrix	State 1	State 3	State 4	
State 2	.2857	.5714	.1429	

The B matrix is the subset of the original matrix consisting of only the transient states.

The F matrix is given by the equation:

$$F = (I-B)^{-1}$$

where I is the identity matrix.

Finally, the FA matrix is the product of the F matrix and the matrix formed by cells that represent going from a transient state to any nontransient state.

Material Requirements Planning

The material requirements planning (MRP) model is used to determine production requirements for items that are dependent.

The Data

Consider the following example:

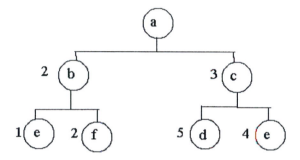

The numbers on the left of each item indicate the number of subcomponents that must be used in the parent component. Lead times are 1 week, except for item *b*, which has a 2-week lead time.

The framework for MRP is given by the number of lines in the indented bill of materials (BOM) and the number of time periods. In the screen, that follows, which represents the preceding example, a problem with 7 BOM lines and 8 periods is displayed. (This is a good module to toggle the [Do not display] **Zeroes** option from the toolbar or **Format** menu.)

Example 1													
Item name	Level	Lead time	# per parent	Onhand inventory	Lot size	Minimum Quantity	pd1	pd2	pd3	pd4	pd5	pd6	pd7	pd8
a		1	1										120	140
b	1	2	2											
e	2	1	1											
f	2	1	2											
c	1	1	3											
d	2	1	5											
e	2	1	4											

Item names. The item names are entered in this column. The same name will appear in more than one row if the item is used by two parent items, such as item *e*. Note that, as a rule, names are unimportant, but in MRP names are extremely important. Case (upper/lower) does not matter, but spaces matter very much.

Item level. The level in the indented BOM must be given here. The item *cannot* be placed at a level more than one below the item immediately above. Do not use low-level codes. Also, please note that it is permissible to have more than one item at level 0 (more than one end item) as shown in Example 2.

Lead time. The lead time in order to get the item is entered here. The default is 1.

Number (#) per parent. The number of units of this subassembly needed for its parent is entered here. The default is 1.

On-hand inventory. The current inventory on-hand at the beginning of the problem is listed here. If a subassembly is listed twice, it makes sense for the current inventory to appear only one time. However, if it appears twice, the starting inventory will be the sum of the listed amounts (see Example 2).

Lot size. The lot size can be specified here. A 0 or a 1 will perform lot-for-lot ordering. If another number is placed here, all orders for that item will be in lots that are integer multiples of that number (see Example 2).

Minimum quantity. It is possible to specify minimum order sizes (see Example 2).

Demands. Demands are entered under Period 1 through Period 8. The demands are entered for *any* level 0 items, in the week in which the items are demanded.

Scheduled receipts. If units are scheduled to be delivered in the future, they should be listed in the appropriate time period (column) and item (row) (see Example 2).

Example 1: A simple MRP example

A sample data screen expressing the problem appears in the preceding illustration. The levels indicate that we have an item termed *a,* which has two (Level 1) subcomponents named *b* and *c.* Subcomponent *b* has two (Level 2) subcomponents named *e* and *f.* Subcomponent *c* has two subcomponents named *d* and *e.* Notice that *e* is a subcomponent of both *b* and *c.*

The demand for the end item, *a,* is 120 units in Week 7 and 140 units in Week 8. The number of subcomponents used is given in the number-per-parent column. For example, end item *a* consists of two subcomponents, *b,* which in turn consists of 1 *e* and 2 *f*s. At the beginning of the problem, there are no units of any kind of inventory on-hand.

MRP Product Tree Viewer

MRP has a product tree viewer, shown as follows. An indented bill of materials is displayed:

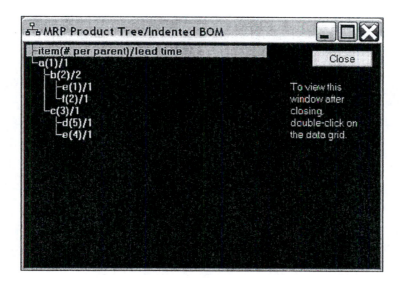

Results

A portion of the results is displayed in the following screen.

Total required. The total number of units required in each week is listed in the first row. For the end item, this is the demand schedule that was input on the data screen. For other items, this is computed.

On-hand. The number on-hand is listed here. This starts as given on the data screen and is reduced according to needs. Example 2 demonstrates on-hand inventory.

Scheduled receipt. This is the amount that was scheduled in the original data screen (see Example 2).

Net required. The net amount required is the amount needed after the on-hand inventory is used. Again, component *c* illustrates the subtraction (see Example 2).

Planned receipt. This is the amount that will be received. It will be the same as the net required many times, but it also may be larger due to minimum order size and lot size requirements (see Example 2).

Order release. This is the net required but offset by the lead time.

🔲 Material Requirements Planning Results										
Example 1 Solution										
Item name (low level)	Pd 0 and before	pd1	pd2	pd3	pd4	pd5	pd6	pd7	pd8	
a (0)										
TOT.REQ.								120	140	
ON HAND										
SchdREC.										
NET REQ								120	140	
PlanREC								120	140	
ORD REL.							120	140		
b (1)										
TOT.REQ.							240	280		
ON HAND										
SchdREC.										
NET REQ							240	280		
PlanREC							240	280		
ORD REL				240	280					
c (1)										
TOT.REQ.							360	420		
ON HAND										
SchdREC.										

Printing

A portion of the printout for the problem is displayed for one main reason: The printout of the input is in a slightly different form than the screen display. Notice that the software prints an indented bill of materials.

```
Ernest Student                    Stat 802/MSOM 806              Howard Weiss
M:\Examples\example1.basic.mat    12-15-2004  13:32:20

Module/submodel: Material Requirements Planning
Problem title: Example 1

Indented BOM and Results ----------

Indented Bill of Materials
Item                          Number per      On hand        Lot Size      Minimum
  ID          Leadtime         parent         Inventory      (if > 1)      quantity
  a              1               1
    b            2               2
      e          1               1
      f          1               2
    c            1               3
      d          1               5
      e          1               4
```

```
Demands for level 0 items

Item Id = a
Period   Demand
1        0
2        0
3        0
4        0
5        0
6        0
7        120
8        140

Scheduled receipts for all items which are not end (level 0) items (if any)

a(low level =  0)
            <= pd 0    pd1      pd2      pd3      pd4      pd5      pd6      pd7    pd8
-------------------------------------------------------------------------------------
TOT.REQ.                                                                     120    140
SchdREC.
ON HAND
NET REQ                                                                      120    140
PlanREC.                                                                     120    140
ORD REL.                                                            120      140

b(low level =  1)
            <= pd 0    pd1      pd2      pd3      pd4      pd5      pd6      pd7    Pd8
-------------------------------------------------------------------------------------
TOT.REQ.                                                            240      280
SchdREC.
ON HAND
NET REQ                                                             240      280
PlanREC.                                                            240      280
ORD REL.                                                   240      280
```

Example 2: MRP options

The next example demonstrates some of the features of the MRP module. The previous example is modified as shown next.

Item name	Level	Lead time	# per parent	Onhand inventory	Lot size	Minimum Quantity	pd1	pd2	pd3	pd4	pd5	pd6	pd7	pd8
a		2	1										120	140
b	1	1	2			300								
e	2	1	1	10										
f	2	1	2		144									
c	1	1	3					800						
d		1	5											65
e	1	1	4	20										

Example 2

First, notice that the level for Product d and the Subcomponent e below it have been changed . Item d is an end item with a demand of 65 in Period 8. Thus e is at Level 2 for a but Level 1 for d. Second, e has been given an initial inventory of both 10 and 20. (We really should not have both but we want to demonstrate what happens.) Third, a scheduled receipt of 800 units in period 2 for item c is included. Fourth, item f must be bought or made in lots that are multiples of 144 units. Fifth, item b must be purchased in quantities of 300 or more.

The results can be seen in the following printout display. Some of the input data has been edited by eliminating some 0's.

```
Lisa B. Ernest
P:\Manual\Examples\Example2.mat        02-20-1999  12:00:52


Module/submodel: Material Requirements Planning
Problem title: Example 2

Indented BOM and Results ----------

Indented Bill of Materials
Item                            Number per    On hand      Lot Size      Minimum
  ID             Lead time         parent     Inventory   (if not lot    quantity
                                                           for lot)

a                    1              1
  b                  2              2                                        300
    e                1              1             10
    f                1              2                        144
  c                  1              3
d                    1              5
  e                  1              4             20


Demands for level 0 items

Item Id = a
Period    Demand
  7         120
  8         140

Item Id = d
Period    Demand
  8         65

Scheduled receipts for all items which are not end (level 0) items (if any)

Item Id = c
Period     Receipt
  2          800
```

```
a(low level =  0)
            <= pd 0   pd1    pd2    pd3    pd4    pd5    pd6    pd7    pd8
--------------------------------------------------------------------------
TOT.REQ.                                                       120    140
ON HAND
SchdREC.
NET REQ                                                        120    140
PlanREC.                                                       120    140
ORD REL.                                                120    140
```

```
d(low level =  0)
            <= pd 0   pd1    pd2    pd3    pd4    pd5    pd6    pd7    pd8
--------------------------------------------------------------------------
TOT.REQ.                                                              65
ON HAND
SchdREC.
NET REQ                                                               65
PlanREC.                                                              65
ORD REL.                                                       65
```

```
b(low level =  1)
          <= pd 0    pd1     pd2     pd3     pd4     pd5     pd6     pd7     pd8
---------------------------------------------------------------------------------
TOT.REQ.                                                    240     280
ON HAND                                                             60      80
SchdREC.
NET REQ                                                     240     220
PlanREC.                                                    300     300
ORD REL.                                  300     300
```

```
c(low level =  1)
          <= pd 0    pd1     pd2     pd3     pd4     pd5     pd6     pd7     pd8
---------------------------------------------------------------------------------
TOT.REQ.                                                    360     420
ON HAND                           800     800     800       800     440     20
SchdREC.                  800
NET REQ
PlanREC.
ORD REL.
```

```
e(low level =  2)
          <= pd 0    pd1     pd2     pd3     pd4     pd5     pd6     pd7     pd8
---------------------------------------------------------------------------------
TOT.REQ.                                          300     300               260
ON HAND   30       30     30      30      30
SchdREC.
NET REQ                                           270     300               260
PlanREC.                                          270     300               260
ORD REL.                                  270     300               260
```

```
f(low level =  2)
          <= pd 0    pd1     pd2     pd3     pd4     pd5     pd6     pd7     pd8
---------------------------------------------------------------------------------
TOT.REQ.                                          600     600
ON HAND                                                   120     96      96      96
SchdREC.
NET REQ                                           600     480
PlanREC.                                          720     576
ORD REL.                                  720     576
```

Notice the on-hand inventory for item *e*. It begins at 30 and remains until it is needed. Notice that for item *c,* a scheduled delivery arrives in Period 2 and then goes into inventory until it is needed. Notice that for item *f* in Period 4, 600 units are needed, but the order is placed for 720 units because it must be a multiple of 144. Notice that for *b* in Period 6, the amount required is 240, but 300 units are ordered because this is the minimum order size.

Networks

Three models are available in this module: minimum spanning tree, shortest path, and maximal flow. The following diagram is used for each of the three examples that follow. In order to start any of the three submodels, it is necessary to indicate the number of branches. In the examples, there are 14 branches. In order to enter each branch, its starting node and its ending node must be given.

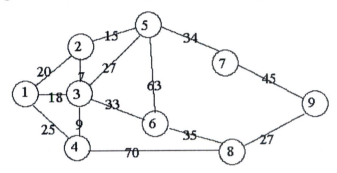

Minimum Spanning Tree

In the minimum spanning tree, we try to connect n nodes to each other using $n - 1$ of the available arcs. Arcs have costs, and the goal is to minimize the total cost. The data and solution to the example appear in the following screen:

Starting node for iterations	Instruction
◄ ► 1	Enter comments on the note. Comments will be se you like.

Branch name	Start node	End node	Cost
	Minimum Spanning Tree Example		
Branch 1	1	2	20
Branch 2	1	3	18
Branch 3	1	4	25
Branch 4	2	3	7
Branch 5	2	5	15
Branch 6	3	4	9
Branch 7	3	5	27
Branch 8	3	6	33
Branch 9	4	8	70
Branch 10	5	6	63
Branch 11	5	7	34
Branch 12	6	8	35
Branch 13	7	9	45
Branch 14	8	9	27

The data is the standard data of the arc or branch, expressed as *from* and *to* node numbers and the cost of using the arc. Above the data is a box that enables the user to specify the starting node number. If you leave it as 0, the lowest node number will be used. Of course, the total cost is independent of the starting node, but the actual arcs used might vary in minimum spanning tree problems.

The eight branches that should be used are marked with a *Y* and the minimum cost of connecting the nine nodes is 178. A table displaying the order in which the branches were added is illustrated in the following screen:

Solution steps

Branch	Starting node	Ending node	Cost	Cumulative cost
		Minimum Spanning Tree Example Solution		
Branch 2	1	3	18	18
Branch 4	2	3	7	25
Branch 6	3	4	9	34
Branch 5	2	5	15	49
Branch 8	3	6	33	82
Branch 11	5	7	34	116
Branch 12	6	8	35	151
Branch 14	8	9	27	178

Shortest Path

A shortest path example follows:

Network type: Undirected / Directed **Origin:** 1 **Destination:** 9 **Instruction:** Enter the name for this branch. Almost any character is permissible.

	Start node	End node	Distance
		Shortest Path	
Branch 1	1	2	20
Branch 2	1	3	18
Branch 3	1	4	25
Branch 4	2	3	7
Branch 5	2	5	15
Branch 6	3	4	9
Branch 7	3	5	27
Branch 8	3	6	33
Branch 9	4	8	70
Branch 10	5	6	63
Branch 11	5	7	34
Branch 12	6	8	35
Branch 13	7	9	45
Branch 14	8	9	27

The goal is to find the shortest path and distance from one point to another. The data screen is shown in the preceding illustration. Notice that it is possible to specify the origin and destination. If you leave it at 0, the program will find the shortest path from the minimum node number to the maximum node number (1 to 9) in this example.

Above the data, the network can be set to be directed or undirected. If it is undirected, the distance from Node *j* to Node *I* is set equal to the distance form Node *I* to Node *j*. For example, the distance from node 2 to node 1 is set to 20.

The solution is as follows:

Networks Results					
Shortest Path Solution					
Total distance = 113		Start node	End node	Distance	Cumulative Distance
Branch 2		1	3	18	18
Branch 8		3	6	33	51
Branch 12		6	8	35	86
Branch 14		8	9	27	113

Four branches should be included in the shortest path, creating the path 1 to3 to 6 to 8 to 9, with a total distance of 113. In addition, the program computes the minimum total distance from every node to every other node as follows. To see the path, set the values for the start and end above the data.

Minimum distance matrix									
Shortest Path Solution									
	1	2	3	4	5	6	7	8	9
1	0	20	18	25	35	51	69	86	113
2	20	0	7	16	15	40	49	75	94
3	18	7	0	9	22	33	56	68	95
4	25	16	9	0	31	42	65	70	97
5	35	15	22	31	0	55	34	90	79
6	51	40	33	42	55	0	89	35	62
7	69	49	56	65	34	89	0	72	45
8	86	75	68	70	90	35	72	0	27
9	113	94	95	97	79	62	45	27	0

Maximal Flow

In this situation, the goal is to maximize the flow from the beginning (source) to the end (sink). The number along each arc represents its capacities, and the second number represents its reverse capacity (capacity in the opposite direction). At the top, the source and sink can be set. If they are left at 0, the source is the node with the lowest number, and the sink is the node with the highest number. Before presenting the solution remember that oftentimes more than one solution exists. Also, there may be more than one way to derive the solution. The maximal flow is 61, and the flows along the branches can be seen in the figure.

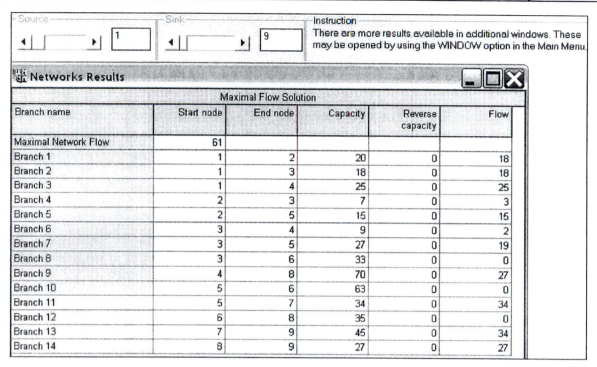

The iterations are given in the following screen. Please note that there are generally several different iteration steps that could be taken to arrive at the same maximal flow.

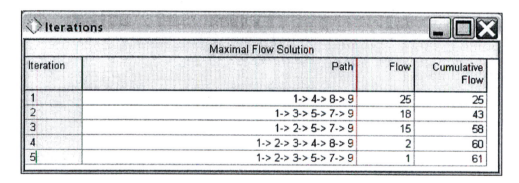

Productivity

Productivity is defined as the ratio of output to input. This software enables you to compute the productivity for any number of inputs and for any number of time periods. The software will compute both the productivity measures for each input and also the changes in productivity from period to period for each input. In addition, the software allows for creating a common denominator so that you will end up with one productivity measure based on multiple inputs. A sample screen that includes both the data and solution appears next. The initialization for this problem requested three inputs (labor hours, material, and inspection hours) and two time periods.

Productivity Results						
Example						
	$/unit (optional)	Period 1	Period 2	Period 1 Productivity	Period 2 Productivity	Productivity Change
Output		10,000	11,000			
Labor hours	8	4,000	5,000	2.5	2.2	down 12%
Material (lbs)	2	5,000	6,000	2	1.83	down 8.33%
Inspection hours	12	1,000	1,000	10	11	up 10%
Aggregated Input ($)		54,000	64,000	.19	.17	down 7.19%

Data

$/unit. This column is used to aggregate all of the inputs into one meaningful measure. Thus, the basic inputs are converted using rates of $8/hour for labor, $2/pound for material, and $12/hour for inspection costs. For example, in Period 1 the aggregate measure is (8 * 4,000) + (2 * 5,000) +(12 * 1,000) = 54,000.

Period 1, 2. The output is entered in the first row, and the inputs are entered in the remaining rows for each period.

Solution

Productivity. For each input, the ratio of output to input is displayed as the productivity for each period. In addition, an aggregate measure is created using the conversion factors in Column 1. Thus, as mentioned previously, the denominator for Period 1 is 54,000 which yields a productivity of 10,000/54,000 or .19 for Period 1.

Change. The last column relates the change from period to period for each of the productivity measures. For example, the aggregate productivity has decreased by 7.19 percent from Period 1 to Period 2.

Project Management

The project scheduling models are used to find the (expected) project completion time for either a Program evaluation and review technique (PERT) problem or a critical path method (CPM) problem. For both networks, either one- or three-time estimate problems can be represented or problems with means and standard deviations for each activity may be entered.

There are five models that are common. These models can be changed without starting anew by using the method box.

Single - Time Estimate and Triple - Time Estimate PERT

Consider a small project given by the following precedence diagram and the table of times that follows the graph.

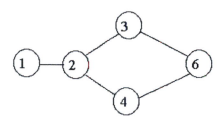

Task	Start Node	End Node	Optimistic	Most Likely	Pessimistic
A	1	2	2	12	25
B	2	3	4	5	6
C	2	4	10	23	28
D	3	6	3	5	7
E	4	6	4	7	9

Data

The following screen contains a triple-time estimate PERT data screen for this example. In PERT representations, the network is defined by giving the starting node and ending node for each task. The network type is given in the box on the left above the data. In this first example, the start node/end node representation for activities is used.

Network type	Method	Instruction
○ Precedence list	Triple time estimate ▼	Enter the value for task 5 for pessimistic time. Any real value is
● Start/end node numbers		permissible.

Example					
	Start node	End node	Optimistic time	Most Likely time	Pessimistic time
Task 1	1	2	2	12	25
Task 2	2	3	4	5	6
Task 3	2	4	10	23	28
Task 4	3	6	3	5	7
Task 5	4	6	4	7	9

The data consists of the following:

Activity name. Activities can be named. In PERT, the name is not used, whereas in CPM (precedence list), the names are critical. In PERT, the "real" name of an activity is given by its starting and ending node labels.

Starting node. The number of the node at which the activity starts is to be given here. Remember, the numbers in a PERT diagram serve as labels rather than numerical values. The labeling is arbitrary. That is, the first node can be 1 or 2 or 90.

Ending node. The number of the node at which the activity ends is to be given here. The number cannot be the same as the starting node number. Two activities cannot have the same pair of starting and ending node numbers. Also, transitivity must be obeyed. That is, an error will occur if laws of transitivity are violated, such as by the pairs (1,2; 2,3; 3,1).

Time estimate. In the single-time problem, it is necessary to give only one time estimate for each task.

Optimistic time. This appears only in the three-time estimate option from the submenu.

Most likely time. This time must be entered in either the one- or three-time estimate version.

Pessimistic time. This appears only in the three-time estimate version.

The Solution

The exact solution screen depends on whether it is a one-estimate or three-estimate problem. In the following screen, a sample three-estimate problem is presented because this contains all of the output information. The one-time estimate problem has less information.

Project Management (PERT/CPM) Results

	Start node	End node	Activity time	Early Start	Early Finish	Late Start	Late Finish	Slack	Standard Deviation
Project			41						4.9385
Task 1	1	2	12.5	0	12.5	0	12.5	0	3.8333
Task 2	2	3	5	12.5	17.5	31	36	18.5	.3333
Task 3	2	4	21.6667	12.5	34.1667	12.5	34.1667	0	3
Task 4	3	6	5	17.5	22.5	36	41	18.5	.6667
Task 5	4	6	6.8333	34.1667	41	34.1667	41	0	.8333

Time. If the three-time estimate version is used, a single time estimate is computed and printed for each activity. The formula used is the traditional formula of

$$t = (a + 4b + c)/6,$$

where a is the optimistic time, b is the most likely time, and c is the pessimistic time. For example, in the screen the time used for Activity 1-2 is

$$[2 + (4 * 12) + 25]/6 = 75/6 = 12.5.$$

Early start (ES). For each activity, its early start is computed. For example, the early start for Activity 3-6 is 17.5. The column named "Activity time" is used for this computation.

Early finish (EF). For each activity, its early finish is computed. In the example, the early finish for Activity 3-6 is 22.5. The early finish is, of course, the early start plus the activity time. For example, the early finish of 3-6 is its early start of 17.5 plus the 5 from the time column.

Late start (LS). For each activity, its late start is computed. In the example, the late start for Activity 3-6 is 36.

Late finish (LF). For each activity, its late finish is computed.

Slack. For each activity, its slack (late start minus early start or late finish minus early finish) is computed. In the example, the slack for Activity 3-6 is:

$$41 - 22.5 = 18.5 \text{ or } 36 - 17.5 = 18.5.$$

Standard deviation. For the three-time estimate model the standard deviation of each activity is listed. The standard deviation is given by pessimistic minus optimistic divided by 6. In the example, the standard deviation of Activity 3-6 is (7 - 3)/6=.67.

Project completion time. The (expected) time at which the project should be completed is given. In the example, this time is 41.

Project standard deviation. If the three-time estimate module is chosen, the project standard deviation is printed. It is computed as the square root of the project variance, which is computed as the sum of the variances of all critical activities.

There is available a table that displays the computations of the tasks' times, standard deviations, and variances, as illustrated in the following screen:

◇ Task time computations								_ ☐ ✕
Example Solution								
	Start node	End node	Optimistic time	Most Likely	'essimistic time	Activity time	Standard Deviation	Variance
Task 1	1	2	2	12	25	12.5	3.8333	14.6944
Task 2	2	3	4	5	6	5	.3333	.1111
Task 3	2	4	10	23	28	21.6667	3	9
Task 4	3	6	3	5	7	5	.6667	.4444
Task 5	4	6	4	7	9	6.8333	.8333	.6944
Project results								
Total of critical								24.3889
Square root of total							4.9385	

It is possible to display Gantt charts for the project, as shown next:

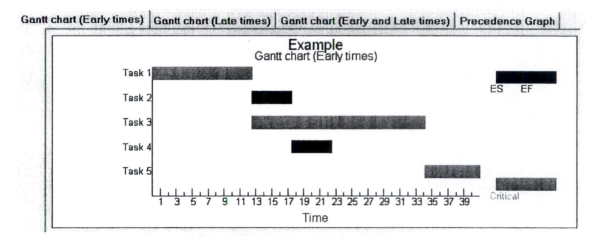

Normal Distribution

Project management is an area where the normal distribution calculator tool is quite useful. The mean (41) and standard deviation (4.93851) from the current example are automatically filled in when the tool is selected. There are several options in terms of what can be computed. For example, the probability of finishing within 50 days or a 95% confidence interval for finishing the project could be computed. Alternatively, we can compute how many days to allow to be 90 percent sure of finishing within that time. We have chosen a 95% confidence interval.

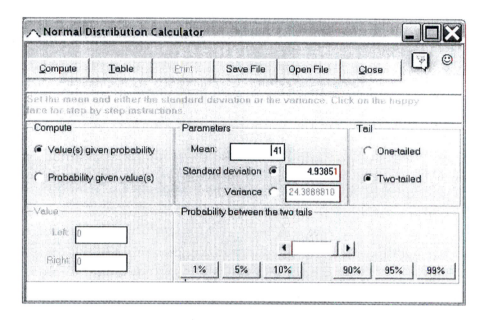

After pressing the **[Compute]** button, the result appears as follows. We are 95 percent confident that the project will be completed in 31 to 51 days.

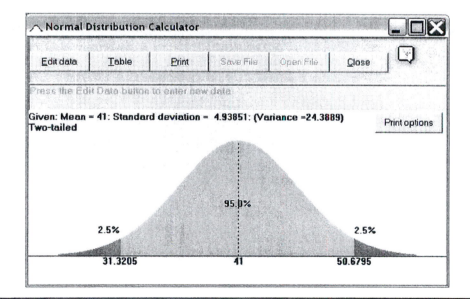

CPM (Precedence List)

The critical path module has the data input in a fashion nearly identical to the assembly line balancing module. Consider the example given in the following table:

Task	Time	Precedences
design	25	
program	30	design
document	22	design
test	10	program
advertise	30	design

The initial data screen appears as follows:

Network type	Method	Instruction
● Precedence list ○ Start/end node numbers	Single time estimate ▼	Enter the value for design for prec 1. Almost any character is permissible.

CPM Example

	Activity time	Prec 1	Prec 2	Prec 3	Prec 4	Prec 5	Prec 6	Prec 7
design	25							
program	30	DESIGN						
document	22	design						
test	10	program						
advertise	30	design						

Task names. Tasks can be given names. The usual naming conventions are true. That is, uppercase and lowercase do not matter but spaces within a name do.

Task times. The task times are entered here.

Predecessors. The predecessors are listed here. Enter one predecessor per spreadsheet cell with up to seven predecessors per activity. It is sufficient to enter only the immediate predecessors.

Rather than displaying the solution to this problem, the precedence graph that the software can display is shown. On the screen, the critical path is displayed in red.

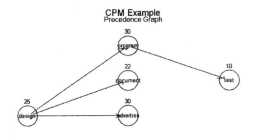

CPM Example
Precedence Graph

Crashing

Following is an example of project management with crashing. The four columns of data are the standard columns for this type of problem – the normal time and normal cost for each activity as well as the crash time and crash cost for each activity. The crash time must be less than or equal to the normal time, and the crash cost must be greater than or equal to the crash cost.

Network type	Method	Instruction
⊙ Precedence list	Crashing ▼	Enter the value for h for prec 7. Almost any character is permissible.
○ Start/end node numbers		

Crashing										
	Normal time	Crash time	Normal Cost	Crash Cost	Prec 1	Prec 2	Prec 3	Prec 4	Prec 5	Prec 6	Prec 7
A	3	2	40	50							
B	6	4	200	300	a						
C	3	2	20	35							
D	2	1	20	32	c						
E	1	1	20	20	a						
F	5	3	150	190	d						
G	7	4	120	150	d	e					
H	4	3	160	195	b	f	g				l

The results are as follows. The software finds the normal time of 16 days and the minimum time of 10 days. For each activity the computer finds the cost of crashing per period (crash cost - normal cost)/(normal time - crash time), which activities should be crashed and by how much, and the prorated cost of crashing.

Project Management (PERT/CPM) Results

Crashing Solution							
	Normal time	Crash time	Normal Cost	Crash Cost	Crash cost/pd	Crash by	Crashing cost
Project	16	10					
A	3	2	40	50	10	1	10
B	6	4	200	300	50	1	50
C	3	2	20	35	15	1	15
D	2	1	20	32	12	1	12
E	1	1	20	20	0	0	0
F	5	3	150	190	20	1	20
G	7	4	120	150	10	3	30
H	4	3	160	195	35	1	35
TOTALS			730				172

A day-by-day crash schedule is available as follows. For example, to reduce the project to 13 days, read across the line with a project time of 13 days. The cost for reducing the project from 14 to 13 days is 12. The total cost of reducing the project from 16 days to 13 days is 32. The activities to crash to achieve 13 days are D by 1 day and G by 2.

Crash schedule

Project time	Period cost	Cumulative cost	A	B	C	D	E	F	G	H
16	0	0								
15	10	10							1	
14	10	20							2	
13	12	32				1			2	
12	25	57	1		1	1			2	
11	35	92	1		1	1			2	1
10	80	172	1	1	1	1		1	3	1

Budgeting

The software has a model for determining the amount of money that will be spent over a project's lifetime. The data is the activity cost as shown next. An early - start budget and a late - start budget can be computed.

Network type	Method	Instruction
● Precedence list ○ Start/end node numbers	Cost Budgeting ▼	Enter the value for f for prec 7. Almost any character is permissible.

Budgeting

	Activity time	Activity Cost	Prec 1	Prec 2	Prec 3	Prec 4	Prec 5	Prec 6	Prec 7
A	5	20							
B	8	17	a						
C	3	19	a						
D	6	23	c						
E	3	25	b						
F	5	15	d						

The regular solution screen is given, but two others are also available. In the next screen, a part of the early-start budget is displayed.

Early Start Budget

Budgeting Solution

	Period 1	Period 2	Period 3	Period 4	Period 5	Period 6	Period 7	Period 8	Period 9	Period 10	Period 11	Period 12
A	4	4	4	4	4							
B						2.125	2.125	2.125	2.125	2.125	2.125	2.125
C						6.3333	6.3333	6.3333				
D									3.8333	3.8333	3.8333	3.8333
E												
F												
Total in Period	4	4	4	4	4	8.4583	8.4583	8.4583	5.9583	5.9583	5.9583	5.9583
Cumulative from	4	8	12	16	20	28.4583	36.9167	45.375	51.3333	57.2917	63.25	69.2083

In addition, the graph contains the early - start and late - start budgets for the entire project.

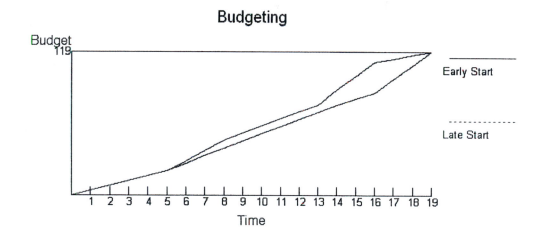

 **Quality Control**

The quality control module can be used for the three major areas of statistical quality control: acceptance sampling, control charts, and process capability. For acceptance sampling, both attributes and variables plans can be developed. Attributes plans are used when the measurement is a defective/nondefective type of measurement, whereas variables plans are used for taking a numerical result rather than simply a yes/no. In addition, the model can be used to compute the producer's and consumer's risk under a given sampling plan or to make a crude plot of the operating characteristic (OC) curve. For control charts, it is possible to develop p-charts for the percentage defective, x-bar charts for the mean, or c-charts for the number of defects. The screens for the first three options are similar, and the screens for the control charts are also similar.

Acceptance Sampling

The exact elements in the data screen depend on whether an attributes sampling plan or a variables sampling plan is selected. In either case, the types of data screens are very similar. The description of the attributes data screen is given first and the variables data screen is presented later.

Example 1: Attributes Sampling

A sample screen that includes both the data and solution appears next:

Quality Control Results				_ □ ✕
Example 1 - Acceptance Sampling Solution				
Parameter	Value		Result	Sampling Plan
AQL	.01		Sample Size	137
LTPD	.05		Critical Value	3
ALPHA	.05		Actual Producer's risk	.0495
BETA	.10		Actual Consumer's risk	.0844

Data

AQL. For acceptance sampling, the acceptable quality level (AQL) must be given. The AQL must be (strictly) greater than 0 and must be less than 1. The interpretation of .01 is an AQL of 1 percent defective.

LTPD. The lot tolerance percent defective (LTPD) must be entered. This has characteristics similar to the AQL. It must be between 0 and 1.

ALPHA – The producer's risk. The probability of a Type 1 error can be set using the drop-down box to be either 1 or 5 percent in attributes sampling. For variables sampling, this entry is numerical, with a maximum allowable value of .99.

BETA – The consumer's risk. The probability of a Type 2 error can be set to be 1, 5, or 10 percent for attributes sampling. This entry is numerical, with a maximum value of .1 for variables sampling.

Solution

A sample problem and solution screen appears in the preceding screen. In this example, the appropriate sampling plan when the AQL is specified at 1 percent, the LTPD is specified at 5 percent, alpha is 5 percent, and beta is 10 percent is determined.

The sample size. The minimum sample size that meets the preceding requirements is determined and displayed. In this example, the appropriate size is 137.

The critical value. The maximum number of defective units (attributes sampling) or the maximum variable average (variables sampling) is displayed. In this example, the maximum allowable number of defects in the 82 units is 3.

Two additional output values appear on the right, indicating that the actual risks differ from the specified risks. The program is designed to find the minimum sample size that meets the requirements. The requirements can be more than met because of the integer nature of the sample size and critical value.

NOTE: The computation of the actual risks is based on the binomial distribution.

Actual producer's risk. The producer's risk in the input is the upper level for the allowable producer's risk. The actual producer's risk can be less and is displayed. In this example, it happens to be .0495, which is nearly the same as the .05 that was set as input.

Actual consumer's risk. The consumer's risk in the input is the upper level for the allowable risk. The actual consumer's risk can be less and is displayed. In this example, it happens to be .0844, which is less than the setting of .1 that was entered as input.

An operating characteristic (OC) Curve can be displayed as illustrated next:

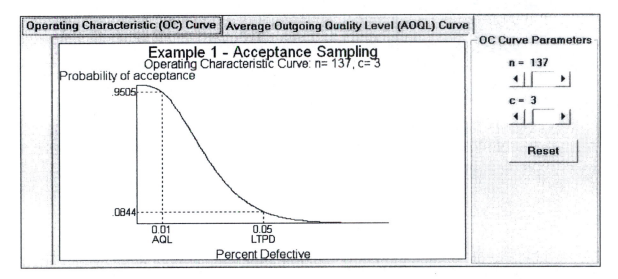

An average outgoing quality (AOQ) Curve is also available.

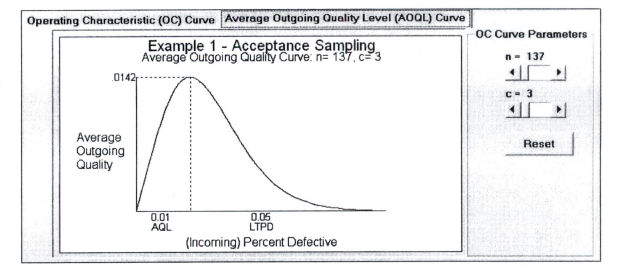

Example 2: Variables sampling

Next the data and output for a variables sampling plan are presented. The lot should be accepted if the mean is 200 pounds but reject the lot if the mean is 180 pounds. The standard deviation of the items produced is 10 pounds. Alpha and beta are 5 percent and 10 percent, respectively. For variables sampling, alpha and beta are numerical rather than preset by the drop-down box. The next example illustrates this more clearly.

Quality Control Results

Example 2: Variables Sampling Example Solution

Parameter	Value		Result	Sampling Plan
U0	200		Sample Size	3
U1	180		Critical Value	189.8964
ALPHA	.04			
BETA	.1			
SIGMA	10			

The output is very similar to the output for attributes sampling. In this example, 3 items should be sampled and weighed. If the average weight is less than 189.8964 pounds, the lot should be rejected.

Control Charts

The fourth, fifth, and sixth options from the submenu are used to develop control charts. Option 4 is used when the percentage of defects is of interest; option 5 when there is a variable measurement and an *x*-bar or range (*R*-bar) chart is required. The last option is for the number of defects (distributed as a Poisson random variable). In any of these cases, it is necessary to indicate how many samples there are.

Example 3: A *p*-bar chart

The module begins by asking for the number of samples. In Example 3, which is shown in the following screen, the number of defects in each of 10 samples has been entered. Also, at the top a 3-sigma control chart is specified and it is indicated that the sample size for each of these samples was 150. Finally, the center line can be specified by using the scrollbar/textbox combination (as in Example 4) or left at 0 as in this example, in which case the software will use the mean.

Method	Sample Size	Center line (0 = use mean)	Instruction
3 sigma (99.73%)	150	0	Enter comments on the note. Comments will be saved with the file and may be printed wit.

Quality Control Results

Example 3: a p-chart solution

Sample	Number of Defects	Fraction Defective		3 sigma (99.73%)
Sample 1	8	.0533	Total Defects	57
Sample 2	5	.0333	Total units sampled	1,500
Sample 3	5	.0333	Defect rate (pbar)	.038
Sample 4	8	.0533	Std dev of proportions	.0156
Sample 5	4	.0267		
Sample 6	5	.0333	UCL (Upper control limit)	.0848
Sample 7	0	0	CL (Center line)	.038
Sample 8	9	.06	LCL (Lower Control Limit)	0
Sample 9	10	.0667		
Sample 10	3	.02		

The program has computed the average percentage of defects, which is displayed as 3.8 percent. The standard deviation of *p*-bar is shown at the upper right as .0156.

A control chart can also be displayed and is exhibited next:

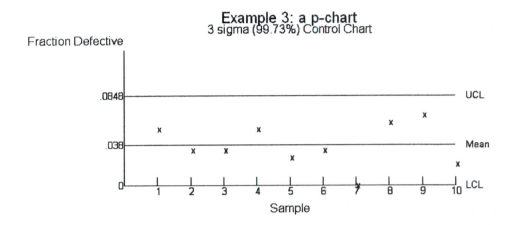

Example 4: An *x*-bar and range chart

After the number of samples is entered, there are two options. Either the raw data can be entered or the mean and range for each sample can be entered. In the example, the data and output for the mean (*x*-bar) and range (*R*-bar) charts are displayed. Six samples of five items have been taken and their weights have been recorded. The first sample had an average weight of 561.9 pounds and a range of 25.3 pounds. The control charts are set up based on the range. (Some authors set up control charts based on standard deviations rather than ranges.) The mean and range chart on the right are based on three standard deviations. Notice that, rather than setting the center line of the mean chart according to the overall mean, it has been set to a specification of 555 using the scrollbar/textbox above the data.

Method	Sample Size	Center line (0 = use mean)	Instruction
3 sigma (99.73%) ▾	◄ ▢ ►	5	◄ ▢ ►	555	There are more results available in additional windows. These may be

Quality Control Results _ □ ✕

			Example 4: An x-bar and range chart solution		
Sample	Mean	Range	3 sigma (99.73%)	X-bar Chart	Range Chart
Sample 1	561.9	25.3	UCL (Upper control limit)	568.021	47.7285
Sample 2	532.1	20	CL (Center line)	555	22.5667
Sample 3	536.1	26.2	LCL (Lower Control Limit)	541.979	0
Sample 4	555.1	18.3			
Sample 5	566.2	28.3			
Sample 6	576.4	17.3			
Averages	554.6333	22.5667			

Example 5: Using raw data in *x*-bar and range charts

The following screen presents the data for an example with raw data:

Method	Center line (0 = use mean)	Instruction
3 sigma (99.73%) ▼	◄ ► 0	Enter the value for item 5 in f. Any non-negative value is permissible.

Example 5: Raw data for x-bar, range charts					
Sample Number	Item 1	Item 2	Item 3	Item 4	Item 5
a	1.23	1.25	1.22	1.21	1.19
b	1.22	1.26	1.2	1.21	1.28
c	1.1	1.23	1.24	1.23	1.2
d	1.2	1.23	1.22	1.23	1.23
e	1.19	1.21	1.19	1.18	1.17
f	1.21	1.22	1.22	1.21	1.22

The software computes the mean and range for each sample and then computes the control charts.

Quality Control Results   _ □ X

Example 5: Raw data for x-bar, range charts solution					
Sample	Mean	Range	3 sigma (99.73%)	X-bar Chart	Range Chart
a	1.22	.06	UCL (Upper control limit)	1.248	.1269
b	1.234	.08	CL (Center line)	1.2133	.06
c	1.2	.14	LCL (Lower Control Limit)	1.1787	0
d	1.222	.03			
e	1.188	.04			
f	1.216	.01			
Averages	1.2133	.06			

Example 6: A *c*-chart

The following screen contains a sample *c*-chart. The number of samples is entered followed by the number of defects in each sample. The program computes and displays the defect rate (4.4), its standard deviation (2.0976), and the control limits.

Quality Control Results

Example 6: a c-chart solution				
Sample	Number of Defects			3 sigma (99.73%)
Sample 1	3		Total Defects	22
Sample 2	5		Total units sampled	5
Sample 3	2		Defect rate (lambda)	4.4
Sample 4	5		Std dev	2.0976
Sample 5	7			
			UCL (Upper control limit)	10.6929
			CL (Center line)	4.4
			LCL (Lower Control Limit)	0

Example 7: Process Capability

For process capability, the upper and lower tolerances for a process must be set. Optionally, the mean may be set. If the mean is not set then the center point between the upper and lower tolerances will be used. Finally, a standard deviation must be given. Both an upper and lower index are computed, and process capability is the minimum of these two indices.

Quality Control Results

Example 7: Process capability solution				
Parameter	Value		Results	Value
Upper tolerance limit	110		Process capability index	.3333
Lower tolerance limit	90		Upper one sided index	.3333
Mean (optional)	105		Lower one sided index	1
Standard deviation	5			

 **Reliability**

The reliability module will compute the reliability of simple systems. If it is used repeatedly, complex systems can be developed. This module can easily be used to determine the appropriate number of backup (standby) pieces of components. The module has five submodels. The general framework for the first three is identical, and the framework for the last two is identical.

Example 1: A basic example

The general framework for reliability is given by the number of simple systems that are in series and the maximum number of components in any simple system. A simple system is a set of parallel components *without* any series. In the following example, a system with four simple systems in series is set up. The largest number of components in any of these four simple systems is six. There is only one type data that needs to be entered.

Component reliability. The required information is the reliability of each component. It is used for computing the reliability of the simple parallel series represented by the column.

NOTE: This is a module where using the option to *not* display zeros ⌀ will make the data display more readable.

Solution

A sample solution screen that also contains the data is given next. Notice that the row in which the probability is entered does not matter, as exemplified by the fact that systems 1 and 2 each have the same reliability of 99 percent.

Reliability Results				
Example 1 Solution				
	Parallel system 1	Parallel system 2	Parallel system 3	Parallel system 4
Component	.99		.9	.96
Backup 1			.8	.96
Backup 2		.99	.8	.92
Backup 3			.7	
Backup 4			.7	
Backup 5			.6	
Prll System Rel	.99	.99	.9999	.9999
Overall Reliability	.9798			

Simple system reliability. Below each parallel system (column), its reliability is presented. The reliability, r, of n components in parallel is given by

$$r = 1 - (1 - r_1)(1 - r_2)...(1 - r_n)$$

where r_j is the reliability of the jth individual component. In the example, the first parallel set has a reliability of its one component, which is .99; the same is true for the second set; the third has an overall reliability of .999856, as listed at the bottom of the third column; and the fourth has a reliability of .999872.

System reliability. The overall system reliability is given at the bottom. The overall reliability is the product of the individual parallel series reliabilities. The example has a system reliability of .979834.

Example 2: Determining the number of backups

It is possible to compute the number of backups required in order to ensure a specified system reliability for a parallel system. For example, suppose that the reliability of an individual component is 50 percent and the desired system reliability is 99 percent. Then, by creating a table with no backups, 1 backup, 2 backups, and so on, the appropriate number of backups can be found. (This is an enumeration method). For the reliabilities specified as 50 percent and 99 percent the appropriate number of components is seven (six backups).

Reliability Results `_ □ X`

	Parallel system 1	Parallel system 2	Parallel system 3	Parallel system 4	Parallel system 5	Parallel system 6	Parallel system 7	Parallel system 8	Parallel system 9	Parallel system 10
					Example 2 Solution					
Component	.5	.5	.5	.5	.5	.5	.5	.5	.5	.5
Backup 1		.5	.5	.5	.5	.5	.5	.5	.5	.5
Backup 2			.5	.5	.5	.5	.5	.5	.5	.5
Backup 3				.5	.5	.5	.5	.5	.5	.5
Backup 4					.5	.5	.5	.5	.5	.5
Backup 5						.5	.5	.5	.5	.5
Backup 6							.5	.5	.5	.5
Backup 7								.5	.5	.5
Backup 8									.5	.5
Backup 9										.5
Prll System Rel	.5	.75	.875	.9375	.9688	.9844	.9922	.9961	.998	.999
Overall Reliability	.2891									

Identical Parallel or Identical Serial Components

Alternatively, a different submodel could be used. The fourth and fifth submodels in the reliability module may be used for computing the reliability of parallel systems with identical components or systems in series with identical components.

Following is a screen for identical parallel components. There are only two items to be entered.

Number in parallel. In the extra data panel above the data table, there is a scrollbar/textbox combination into which the number of components is placed. In this example, we are indicating that there are 10 identical components (one original and nine backups).

Component reliability. The data table requires one piece of information. This is the reliability of the components. In the example, .5 indicates that each of the 10 parallel components has a reliability of 50 percent.

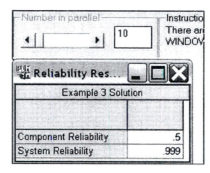

Solution

The solution indicates that the overall reliability is .999023, which agrees with the more detailed display in the previous screen in Column 10.

Simulation

The simulation model is used to generate values from discrete probability distributions or frequency tables. Up to 10 categories can be simulated, and up to 10,000 numbers can be generated in each experiment. The number and percentage of occurrences of each category are displayed, and the generation of the numbers can be viewed on a step-by-step basis.

In order to generate a simulation problem, it is necessary to provide the number of categories for the data. The following screen has both the data and solution for a simulation of 10 categories.

Number of trials		Seed		Instruction
◄	50	◄	3	There are more results available in additional windows. These may be opened by using the WINDOW option in the Main Menu.

Simulation Results ▫☐✕

Example Solution								
Category name	Value	Frequency	Probability	Cumulative Probability	Value * Frequency	Occurrences	Percentage	Occurences * Value
category 1	1	1	.03	.03	.03	1	.02	1
category 2	2	8	.21	.23	.41	11	.22	22
category 3	3	3	.08	.31	.23	3	.06	9
category 4	4	4	.1	.41	.41	3	.06	12
category 5	5	2	.05	.46	.26	0	0	0
category 6	6	5	.13	.59	.77	6	.12	36
category 7	7	8	.21	.79	1.44	10	.2	70
category 8	8	7	.18	.97	1.44	13	.26	104
category 9	9	1	.03	1	.23	3	.06	27
category 10	10	0	0	1	0	0	0	0
Total		39	1	Expected	5.21	50	1	281
							Average	5.62

The elements of data are as follows:

The number of trials. This is the number of random numbers to be generated. Up to 10,000 trials can be generated.

Seed. When using simulation, a seed for the random number generator must be given. The default seed for the computer is 0. If you use the same seed or row or column two times, the same set of random numbers will be generated. In other words, to run different experiments you must reset the random number generation process by changing the seed.

NOTE: For Heizer/Render, Taylor, or Render/Stair/Hanna users, the following random number generation method is available:

Random number generation method. There are two basic ways that the random numbers can be generated. It is possible to have the software generate random numbers and then convert them to the desired frequencies, or it is possible to use the random numbers from a table in a book.

Value. The values for the variables are given here. In the example, they are 1 through 10, but they can be any set of values. They are used for the computation of the expected value.

Category frequencies. The frequencies for each category are entered here. These must be non-negative but do not need to be integers, nor do they need to sum to anything special (such as 1 or 100), because the program will total this column and scale the results.

Example: Simulating a frequency table

The preceding screen displays a 10-category problem and its solution. At the top, it can be seen that for 50 trials are used, with the computer generating random numbers and the seed being 3. The solution includes the following:

Total. This is the total of the frequency column and as mentioned previously, is used for scaling. In this case, divide the frequencies by 39 in order to determine the relative frequencies or probabilities.

Probability. This column represents the scaled frequency for each category given by the frequency divided by the total frequency. For example, Category 2 has a relative frequency of 8 divided by 39, or 20.51 percent.

Cumulative probability. The cumulative probability is needed to convert the uniform random number from the computer or book to the appropriate relative frequency. The cumulative probability is simply the running sum of probabilities. For example, the cumulative probability for category 3 is .0256 + .2051 + .0769 = .3077.

Value * frequency. This column is used to compute the weighted average or expected value of the given frequency distribution. In this example, the column total is 5.2051, which is the weighted average of the two columns, or the expected value of the distribution.

Occurrences. This is the count of the number of times this category was generated. The individual occurrences can be seen by displaying the history. In this experiment, Category 4 was generated three times.

Percentage. This is the occurrences divided by the total number of trials. For example, the three occurrences of Category 4 represent 6 percent of the total of 50 trials.

*Occurrences * value*. This column is used to compute the weighted average of the simulated frequency distribution. In this example, the column total is 281, which, divided by the 50 runs, yields a weighted average of 5.62.

A list of the 50 individual numbers can be displayed.

Individual Runs

Example Solution

Number	Random Number	Category
1	.37	category 4
2	.53	category 6
3	1	category 9
4	.73	category 7
5	.77	category 7
6	.07	category 2
7	.59	category 6
8	.4	category 4
9	.1	category 2
10	.9	category 8
11	.2	category 2
12	.58	category 6
13	.47	category 6
14	.11	category 2
15	.02	category 1
16	.86	category 8
17	.84	category 8
18	1	category 9
19	.89	category 8

The first uniform number generated was .37, and this falls between .3077 and .4103, the cumulative for Category 4, so Category 4 is chosen. The second random number generated was .5337, and this falls between .4615 and .5897, so Category 6 is designated.

 **Statistics**

The statistics module is used to compute the mean (or expected value or weighted average) and standard deviation of a sample or population or a frequency table or a probability distribution. In addition, normal distribution calculators may be performed using this module. The normal distribution calculator tool, displayed in the project management section performs the same calculations as this model. It has a slightly better input design (because it is not restricted to being a table) but it cannot save files as this module can.

When creating a data set you will be asked in the lower left corner of the creation screen about the type of data set that you want. Examples for each of the types are provided.

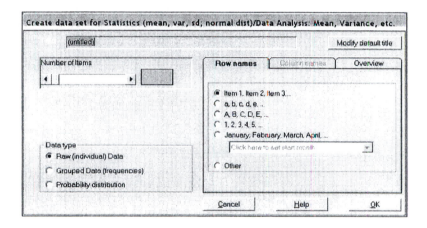

Example 1: Computing statistics for raw data

Following is a sample screen that includes a list of 5 items.

Value. The first column contains the numerical values (x_i)

The next two columns display the computations that are used for the variance and standard deviation. The last column displays the data in sorted order.

The results include the mean, median, mode, population (divide by n) and sample (divide by $n - 1$) variances and standard deviations, the minimum, maximum and range. There also is a graph available and a histogram that can be computed for the data.

Statistics (mean, var, sd; normal dist) Results					
Example 1: Raw data solution					
	Value	(xi-xbar)	(xi-xbar)^2		Sorted data
Item 1	18	-17.8	316.84		15
Item 2	34	-1.8	3.24		18
Item 3	25	-10.8	116.64		25
Item 4	87	51.2	2,621.44		34
Item 5	15	-20.8	432.64		87
Totals	179		3,490.8		
Statistics					
Mean	35.8				
Median	25				
Mode	More than 1				
Population variance	698.16				
Population standard deviation	26.4227				
Sample variance	872.7				
Sample standard deviation	29.5415				
Minimum	15				
Maximum	87				
Range	72				

Example 2: Computing statistics for a frequency table

In the following example, grouped data is entered.

Statistics (mean, var, sd; normal dist) Results							
Example 2: Frequencies Solution							
Class Interval	Midpoint or value, xi	Frequency, fi	Percent	Val * Freq, xi * fi	xi-xbar	(xi-xbar)^2	(xi-xbar)^2*fi
90-99	94.5	218	.1446	20,601	13.4549	181.0346	39,465.54
80-89	84.5	643	.4264	54,333.5	3.4549	11.9364	7,675.108
70-79	74.5	570	.378	42,465	-6.5451	42.8382	24,417.77
60-69	64.5	62	.0411	3,999	-16.5451	273.74	16,971.88
50-59	54.5	15	.0099	817.5	-26.5451	704.6418	10,569.63
Totals		1,508	1	122,216			99,099.92
Statistics							
Mean	81.0451						
Population variance	65.7161						
Population standard	8.1065						
Sample variance	65.7597						
Sample standard deviation	8.1092						

Midpoint or value. This is the value to be used for computations.

Frequency or probability. The frequencies for each category are entered here. These must be nonnegative but do not need to be integers, nor do they need to sum to anything special (such as 1 or 100), because the program will total this column and scale the results.

Total. This is the total of the frequency column and, as mentioned previously, is used for scaling.

Percent. This column represents the scaled frequency for each category, given by the frequency divided by the total frequency.

*Value * frequency.* This column is used to compute the weighted average or expected value of the given frequency distribution. In this example, the column total is 122,216, which is divided by the number of observations (1,508) to derive the mean of 81.0451.

xi - xbar. In order to compute the standard deviation we need to compute the values x_i minus x bar.

(xi - xbar)^2. The previous value is squared.

*(xi - xbar^2) * fi.* The squared values are weighted by the probabilities and summed.

Example 3: Computing statistics for a probability distribution

Both the data and the results are on the results screen that follows.

Statistics (mean, var, sd, normal dist) Results

Example 3: A Probability Distribution Solution

Outcome	Value, k	Probability Pr(X = k)	Cum Prob, Pr(X <= k)	Value*Prob, k*Pr(X = k)	k-mu	(k-mu)^2	(k-mu)^2 * Pr(X = k)
Outcome 1	1	.4	.4	.4	-1.3	1.69	.676
Outcome 2	2	.25	.65	.5	-.3	.09	.0225
Outcome 3	3	.15	.8	.45	.7	.49	.0735
Outcome 4	4	.1	.9	.4	1.7	2.89	.289
Outcome 5	5	.05	.95	.25	2.7	7.29	.3645
Outcome 6	6	.05	1	.3	3.7	13.69	.6845
Totals		1		2.3			2.11
Statistics							
Mean	2.3						
Variance	2.11						
Standard deviation	1.4526						

Value. This is the value to be used for computations.

Probability. The probabilities for each category are entered here. These must be nonnegative and must sum to 1.

Total. This is the total of the probability column and should total 1.

Cumulative. The cumulative probability is presented. The cumulative probability is simply the running sum of probabilities. For example, the cumulative probability for value 3 is .4 + .25 + .15 = .8.

Value * probability. This column is used to compute the weighted average or expected value of the given frequency distribution. In this example, the column total is 2.3, which is the weighted average of the two columns or the expected value or mean of the distribution.

k - mu. In order to compute the standard deviation we need to compute the values x_i minus x bar.

(k - mu)^2. The previous value is squared.

(k - mu)^2 * Pr(x = k). The squared values are weighted by the probabilities and summed. The variance for this data is 2.11

Example 4: The Normal Distribution

You need to indicate on the creation screen whether you want to compute cutoffs given a probability or compute probabilities given a cutoff or cutoffs

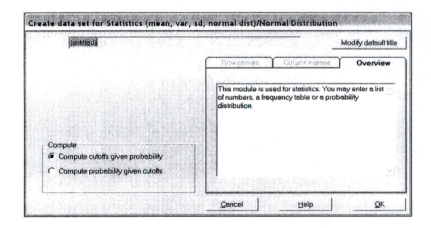

In the project management example the cutoffs were given to create a 95% probability so in this example we will compute the probability given cutoffs. The data and the results appear in the results screen.

▦ Statistics (mean, var, sd; no... ▭ ▢ ✕		
Example 4: A Normal Distribution example solution		
Parameter		Value
Mean		27
Standard deviation		1.3
Left cutoff		24
Right cutoff		28
Results		
Probability to the left of the tail		1.05%
Probability in the center		76.86%
Probability to the right of the tail		22.09%

Once again, a graph is available.

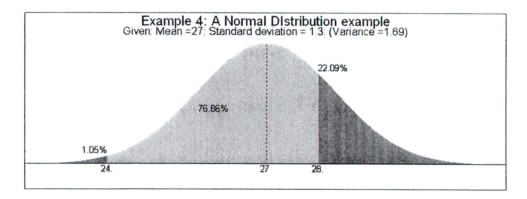

NOTE: The normal calculator from the Tools menu can perform the same computations. The User Interface for the calculator is a little more intuitive to use than the tabular input here.

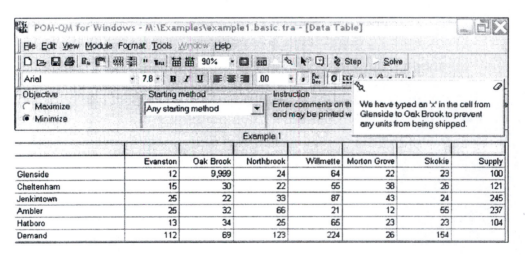 The Transportation Model

This module is used to solve transportation problems. Of course, this module can be used to solve other problems, such as assignment problems and production planning problems, as well.

NOTE: The aggregate planning module contains a transportation option.

Data

The transportation problem is structured according to the number of origins in the problem and the number of destinations.

Objective function. Although minimization is the usual objective in transportation, either minimize or maximize can be chosen at the time that the data set is created or, as usual at the edit screen, through the objective box above the data set.

Consider the following example. The initial data screen for this 5-by-6 sample problem follows:

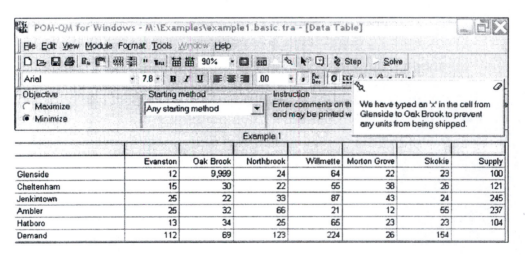

Notice that a STEP button appears on the toolbar.

Objective. The objective function can be changed in the usual option method.

Shipping costs. The main body of information is the shipping cost from each origin to each destination.

NOTE: If you enter an 'x' for a cell, then a large shipping cost ($9,999/unit) will be placed in the cell, which will effectively eliminate the cell from consideration in the solution.

Supplies. The column on the far right contains the supply at each origin.

Demands. The demand row contains the demand at each destination.

Starting method. Four options are available in the method drop-down box. They are as follows:

1. Any method (the software actually uses Vogel's approximation method)
2. Northwest corner method
3. Vogel's approximation method
4. Minimum cost method (also known as the intuitive method)

The optimal cost is, of course, independent of the initial method, as is the optimal shipping schedule when there are no alternative solutions.

Solution

A solution to the sample problem follows. The main solution screen shows the shipments that are to be made and contains the total cost in the upper-left corner. If a dummy row or column needs to be added, it will appear in this table.

Total cost or profit. The total cost or profit appears in the upper-left corner.

Transportation Shipments							
Example 1 Solution							
Optimal cost = $14,364	Evanston	Oak Brook	Northbrook	Willmette	Morton Grove	Skokie	Dummy
Glenside	100						
Cheltenham			121				
Jenkintown		69				77	99
Ambler				224	13		
Hatboro	12		2		13	77	

Marginal costs

A table of marginal costs is available.

Marginal Costs							_ □ ✕
Example 1 Solution						
	Evanston	Oak Brook	Northbrook	Willmette	Morton Grove	Skokie	Dummy
Glenside		9,979	0	33	0	1	2
Cheltenham	5	12		26	18	6	4
Jenkintown	11		7	54	19		
Ambler	23	22	52			43	12
Hatboro		13		33			1

Stepping

The same problem is considered next but the solution method is changed to Northwest corner. The first table appears as follows:

Transportation Shipments							_ □ ✕
Example 1 Shipments NOTE:Dummy column has been added						
Cost =31,087	Evanston	Oak Brook	Northbrook	Willmette	Morton Grove	Skokie	Dummy
Glenside	100	(9,972)	(5)	(-9)	(-42)	(-84)	(-84)
Cheltenham	12	69	40	(-21)	(-29)	(-84)	(-87)
Jenkintown	(-1)	(-19)	83	162	(-35)	(-97)	
Ambler	(65)	(57)	(99)	62	26	149	(-32)
Hatboro	(85)	(91)	(90)	(76)	(43)	5	99

Notice that some of the numbers are enclosed in parentheses whereas others are not. (On the screen the numbers also display in two different colors.) The numbers without a sign represent the shipments, whereas the numbers with a sign represent the marginal costs. The largest (absolute value) marginal cost is -98 in the cell Jenkintown to Dummy (which is the current cell selected by the software). Also notice that the total cost, which is $31,087, is displayed at the top of the table. You do not have to use the entering cell suggested by the software. You can use the direction keys to change the entering cell.

Repeating this process five more times brings the screen displayed next. In this screen, there is a message after the cost indicating that the solution is optimal and that FINISH should be pressed. Everything after this is as before if we press a key one more time. That is, we can display the shipments, the marginal costs, or both in one table.

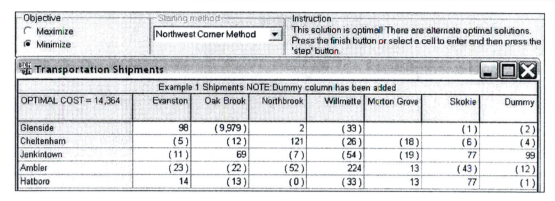

Another optimal solution is given by stepping again.

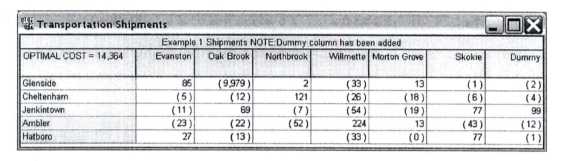

Waiting Lines

There are many different waiting line situations that are described in POM and QM textbooks. Standard models include single-phase queueing models that do not allow feedback, batch arrivals, batch service, balking, or reneging. Models of this type are described by a standard notation termed Kendall's notation, although many textbooks avoid this very common notation.

Some queueing models allow for the determination of the average cost of operating a queueing system, where the cost is the sum of the labor costs and the waiting costs are charged against either the system time (number in system) or the waiting time (number waiting).

Data

The framework for waiting lines depends on the specific model used. Nine models are considered here, and each of these models can be used with or without costs. In general, the exact data required will vary as the model changes. The models are chosen at the beginning.

Nine models are available. Some models are special cases of other models. In particular, all of the single-server models are special cases of the corresponding multiple-server models. The models are listed below with their aliases. All models assume a Poisson arrival process.

> $M/M/1$ – Exponential service times, 1 server (the single server model)
> $M/D/1$ – Constant service times, 1 server (the constant service model)
> $M/G/1$ – General service times, 1 server
> $M/E_k/1$ – Erlang-k service times, 1 server
> $M/M/s$ – Exponential service times, 1 or more servers (the multiple server model)
> $M/M/1$ with a finite queue (or finite system) size
> $M/M/s$ with a finite queue (or finite system) size
> $M/M/1$ with a finite population
> $M/M/s$ with a finite population

The first parameter in the notation refers to the arrival process. The M stands for Memorylessness, which means a Poisson arrival process. The second parameter refers to the service process. The M again stands for memoryless, which means that the service times follow an exponential distribution. The D stands for deterministic, which is used when service times are constant (always the same). The *G* stands for general, and the E_k stands for Erlang-*k* distribution. The third parameter is the number of servers (also called channels). Note that *s* can be set to 1 in the *M/M/s* models to solve the *M/M/1* models.

Data

A sample data screen appears next.

Cost analysis	Time unit (arrival, service rate)	Instruction
⊙ No costs ○ Use Costs	hours ▾	Enter the value for the service rate(mu). This must be a strictly positive value.

Example 1: The M/M/1 queue		
Parameter	**Value**	
M/M/1 (exponential service times)		
Arrival rate(lambda)	26	
Service rate(mu)	30	
Number of servers	1	

Arrival rate (lambda). Every queueing system must have a customer arrival rate. This number is a *rate,* which means that a time unit (hour, day, etc.) is associated with the arrival rate. This is critical because the time unit must match the time unit of the next parameter.

Service rate (mu). The number to be entered is the rate at which individual servers process customers. Note that this is a *rate*. That is, it is common to know the service *time*. But this time must be converted to a rate *and the time unit of this rate must match the time unit of the arrival rate.*

Number of servers. The minimum and default value for the number of servers is 1. There are other input parameters for the other models that are explained in the examples.

Time unit. There is a drop-down box for the time unit. This serves two purposes. First, it reminds you that the arrival rate and service rate must both be based on the same time unit. Second, if you select hours, the output display will show "minutes" and "seconds." If not, the output display will show "60 * times answer."

Example 1: The *M/M/1* model

Customers arrive at a rate of 26 per hour according to a Poisson arrival process. There is one server who serves customers in an average time of 2 minutes according to an exponential distribution.

The output screen for this system follows. Notice that the arrival rate is entered as 26, as given in the problem statement. The service time of 2 minutes must be converted to a rate of 30 per hour.

Parameter	Value		Parameter	Value	Minutes	Seconds
M/M/1 (exponential service			Average server utilization	.8667		
Arrival rate(lambda)	26		Average number in the queue(Lq)	5.6333		
Service rate(mu)	30		Average number in the system(Ls)	6.5		
Number of servers	1		Average time in the queue(Wq)	.2167	13	780
			Average time in the system(Ws)	.25	15	900

Waiting Lines Results — Example 1: The M/M/1 queue solution

Average server utilization. This is the percentage of time that each server is busy on average. In the example, the one server is busy 87 percent of the time.

Average number in the queue (line). This is the average number of customers who are in the system waiting for service. That is, they have not yet begun their service. In the example, there are 5.63 customers waiting, on average.

Average number of customers in the system. This is the average number of customers who either are in line or are being served. In the example, there are 6.5 customers in the system, on average.

Average time in the queue (line). This is the average time that a customer spends waiting before service begins. The time unit is the same as that of the arrival and service rates. In the example, it is .2167 *hours*.

Average time in the system. This is the average time that a customer spends waiting *and* being served. In the example it is .25 *hours*

Many times we want to convert the average waiting and system times from hours to minutes or from minutes to seconds. The average times will be multiplied by 60 or 3,600, and the answers will show beside the original averages. The numbers there express the same time but with a unit of *minutes,* because the original times were in hours.

The probabilities (percentage of time) of exactly k customers in the system, the cumulative probabilities of k or fewer customers being in the system, and the decumulative probability of strictly more than k customers in the system can be displayed. The screen will appear as follows. For example, the probability that exactly three customers are in the system is .0868, whereas the probability that three or fewer customers are in the system is .4358. The probability that (strictly) more than three customers are in the system is .5642. Note that these probabilities are available for all models that have exponential (memoryless) service times.

Table of Probabilities

Example 1: The M/M/1 queue solution

k	Prob (num in sys = k)	Prob (num in sys <= k)	Prob (num in sys >k)
0	.1333	.1333	.8667
1	.1156	.2489	.7511
2	.1001	.349	.651
3	.0868	.4358	.5642
4	.0752	.5111	.4889
5	.0652	.5762	.4238
6	.0565	.6327	.3673
7	.049	.6817	.3183
8	.0424	.7242	.2758
9	.0368	.7609	.2391
10	.0319	.7928	.2072
11	.0276	.8204	.1796
12	.0239	.8444	.1556
13	.0207	.8651	.1349
14	.018	.8831	.1169
15	.0156	.8987	.1013
16	.0135	.9122	.0878
17	.0117	.9239	.0761
18	.0101	.9341	.0659

Example 2: The *M/D/1* model

In the next example shown in the following screen, the data is the same as in the previous example but the model has been changed.

Waiting Lines Results

Example 2: M/D/1 Example Solution

Parameter	Value	Parameter	Value	Minutes	Seconds
M/D/1 (constant service times)		Average server utilization	.8667		
Arrival rate(lambda)	26	Average number in the queue(Lq)	2.8167		
Service rate(mu)	30	Average number in the system(Ls)	3.6833		
Number of servers	1	Average time in the queue(Wq)	.1083	6.5	390
		Average time in the system(Ws)	.1417	8.5	510

The output format is the same. Because the model has changed, some of the results have changed. In particular, the number of customers in line is 2.8167 rather than the 5.63 from the *M/M/1* system. (The number in line and the time in line in a *M/D/1* system are always half of those in an *M/M/1* system.) Probabilities are not available because the service times are not exponential.

Example 3: The *M/G/1* model

In this model, service times may have any distribution. The input to the routine is not only the mean service rate but also the standard deviation of the service *time*. The following screen contains all of the information for this example. Notice that there is one extra row for the input. The output is the same. In the example, the mean rate is still 30 customers per hour, as before, but the service time standard deviation is .05 *hours* or 3 minutes.

Waiting Lines Results					
Example 3: The M/G/1 Model Solution					
Parameter	Value	Parameter	Value	Minutes	Seconds
M/G/1 (general service times)		Average server utilization	.8667		
Arrival rate(lambda)	26	Average number in the queue(Lq)	9.1542		
Service rate(mu)	30	Average number in the system(Ls)	10.0208		
Number of servers	1	Average time in the queue(Wq)	.3521	21.125	1,267.5
Standard deviation	.05	Average time in the system(Ws)	.3854	23.125	1,387.5

All service distributions are a special case of the general distribution. A standard deviation of 1/rate yields the exponential distribution. For example, because the service rate is 30, if the service time standard deviation is 1/30 = .03333, the model has an exponential service time distribution.

Waiting Lines Results					
Example 3b: Exponential Service Times Expressed as an M/G/1 Queue Solution					
Parameter	Value	Parameter	Value	Value * 60	Value * 60 * 60
M/G/1 (general service times)		Average server utilization	.8667		
Arrival rate(lambda)	26	Average number in the queue(Lq)	5.6333		
Service rate(mu)	30	Average number in the system(Ls)	6.5		
Number of servers	1	Average time in the queue(Wq)	.2167	13	779.9993
Standard deviation	.0333	Average time in the system(Ws)	.25	15	899.9993

The exponential service time model is expressed as a general service time model in the preceding screen. Notice that the answers are identical to those in Example 1 except for roundoff (because we used .0333 rather than 1/30th exactly).

A standard deviation of 0 in the general service time model will yield the constant service time (*M/D/1*) model. Compare the next screen to the results of Example 2.

Waiting Lines Results

Example 3c: Constant Service Times Expressed as an M/G/1 Queue Solution					
Parameter	Value	Parameter	Value	Value * 60	Value * 60 * 60
M/G/1 (general service times)		Average server utilization	.8667		
Arrival rate(lambda)	26	Average number in the queue(Lq)	2.8167		
Service rate(mu)	30	Average number in the system(Ls)	3.6833		
Number of servers	1	Average time in the queue(Wq)	.1083	6.5	390
Standard deviation	0	Average time in the system(Ws)	.1417	8.5	510

Example 4: The $M/E_k/1$ model

Another available service time distribution is the Erlang-k distribution. The following screen exhibits the $M/E_k/1$ model and solution. The only difference in the input is that the value for k must be given (rather than no value or a standard deviation).

Waiting Lines Results

Example 4: Erlang service times solution					
Parameter	Value	Parameter	Value	Minutes	Seconds
M/Ek/1 (Erlang-k service times)		Average server utilization	.8667		
Arrival rate(lambda)	26	Average number in the queue(Lq)	3.7556		
Service rate(mu)	30	Average number in the system(Ls)	4.6222		
Number of servers	1	Average time in the queue(Wq)	.1444	8.6667	520
k for Erlang-k	3	Average time in the system(Ws)	.1778	10.6667	640

When k is 1, as in the following screen, the model is an exponential distribution. Compare the results that follow with the first example.

Waiting Lines Results

Example 4b: Exponential service times expressed as Erlang distribution solution					
Parameter	Value	Parameter	Value	Minutes	Seconds
M/Ek/1 (Erlang-k service times)		Average server utilization	.8667		
Arrival rate(lambda)	26	Average number in the queue(Lq)	5.6333		
Service rate(mu)	30	Average number in the system(Ls)	6.5		
Number of servers	1	Average time in the queue(Wq)	.2167	13	780
k for Erlang-k	1	Average time in the system(Ws)	.25	15	900

Example 5: The $M/M/s$ queue

The most basic question in queueing is what will happen if the number of servers is increased. In the following screen the output for the original situation is presented, except with two servers. Waiting time is now .0077 hours rather than the .217 hours in the original description. To double check the original example, use the M/M/s model and enter 1 server.

Waiting Lines Results					
Example 5: Multiple servers solution					
Parameter	Value	Parameter	Value	Minutes	Seconds
M/M/s		Average server utilization	.4333		
Arrival rate(lambda)	26	Average number in the queue(Lq)	.2004		
Service rate(mu)	30	Average number in the system(Ls)	1.067		
Number of servers	2	Average time in the queue(Wq)	.0077	.4624	27.7428
		Average time in the system(Ws)	.041	2.4624	147.7428

Example 6: The *M/M/1* system with a finite queue

In this system, the number of waiting spaces is finite. The typical example is a telephone system. The extra line of input to this model is the maximum allowable system size. Notice that the *system* is required not the *waiting line* size. In the following example at most two customers can be in the system. This means that no more than one can be waiting with the second being served. (This is a single-line phone with call waiting.) If there were two servers, it would mean that no one can be waiting. Be careful when considering the system size versus the waiting area size.

NOTE: The model is termed a *finite queue* but it is the system size, not the queue size, that is entered into the program.

Because the system size is limited, it is possible that customers will arrive at the system but be blocked from entering. Therefore, define the effective arrival rate as the actual number of customers who enter the store rather than all of those who arrive at the store. Furthermore, the output displays the percentage of time (probability) that the system is full.

Waiting Lines Results					
Example 6: Finite system size model solution					
Parameter	Value	Parameter	Value	Minutes	Seconds
M/M/1 with a Finite System		Average server utilization	.618		
Arrival rate(lambda)	26	Average number in the queue(Lq)	.2869		
Service rate(mu)	30	Average number in the system(Ls)	.9049		
Number of servers	1	Average time in the queue(Wq)	.0155	.9286	55.7143
Maximum system size	2	Average time in the system(Ws)	.0488	2.9286	175.7143
		Effective Arrival Rate	18.5399		
		Probability that system is full	.2869		

In the example, only 71 percent of the customers who show up enter the system, customers show up at a rate of 26 per hour but the effective arrival rate is 18.539 per hour. When the probabilities are displayed as follows, it can be seen that 28.69 percent of the time the system is full ($k = 2$). That is, 28.69 percent of the time, when a phone call is made it receives a busy signal.

k	Prob (num in sys = k)	Prob (num in sys <= k)	Prob (num in sys >k)
	Example 6: Finite system size model solution		
0	.382	.382	.618
1	.3311	.7131	.2869
2	.2869	1	0

Example 7: The *M/M/1* system with a finite population

Typically it is assumed that the population is infinite. The following screen exhibits a population of 13 potential customers, *each* arriving at a rate of 2 times per hour (for a net potential arrival rate of 26, as in the previous examples). This is the arrival rate when they are not in the system. However, from the output it can be seen that each customer averages .088 hours each time he or she arrives. The effective arrival rate is the 1 arrival per hour times the average number of the 13 who are not in the system. In this example, the effective arrival rate is only 22.1 customers per hour (rather than the potential of 26 arrivals per hour). If service were better, then these customers could arrive more frequently. The screen includes the probability that a customer waits. (This is *not* the probability that all servers are busy, because arrival rates vary depending on the number in the system.)

NOTE: In this model, the arrival rate to be entered into the program is the arrival rate *for an individual customer*. In many textbooks, the time between arrivals is given. This time must be converted to an arrival rate. For example, it might be that each of 5 customers shows up on average every 30 minutes. This must be converted to a rate of 60/30 = 2 per hour (per customer). The program will automatically adjust for the number of customers. Notice that we enter the number 2 as the arrival rate. It is tempting to enter 2 * 5 =10, but this is incorrect!

Waiting Lines Results _ □ X

Example 7: Finite Population Model Solution					
Parameter	Value	Parameter	Value	Minutes	Seconds
M/M/1 with a Finite Population		Average server utilization	.7368		
Arvl rt PER CUSTOMER	2	Average number in the queue(Lq)	1.2115		
Service rate(mu)	30	Average number in the system(Ls)	1.9483		
Number of servers	1	Average time in the queue(Wq)	.0548	3.2888	197.3262
Population size	13	Average time in the system(Ws)	.0881	5.2888	317.3262
		Effective Arrival Rate	22.1034		
		Probability that customer waits	.6904		

Example 8: The *M/M/s* queue with costs

The next screen contains an example with costs. Customer costs can be charged against either the time a customer spends in the system or charged against only the time waiting. The charge is $2 for each hour the customer waits. This yields a total cost of $2 * 6.5 customers in the system plus the $4/ hour labor cost for a total system cost of $17 per hour (bottom line in table). Alternatively, the charge might be against the time a customer waits. In this case, we have 5.633 customers waiting on average multiplied by $2 for a subtotal of $11.26 to which we add the $4 server charge yielding $15.27, as displayed in the second line from the bottom.

Waiting Lines Results _ □ X

Example 8: Costing Solution					
Parameter	Value	Parameter	Value	Minutes	Seconds
M/M/s		Average server utilization	.8667		
Arrival rate(lambda)	26	Average number in the queue(Lq)	5.6333		
Service rate(mu)	30	Average number in the system(Ls)	6.5		
Number of servers	1	Average time in the queue(Wq)	.2167	13	780
Server cost $/time	4	Average time in the system(Ws)	.25	15	900.0001
Waiting cost $/time	2	Cost (Labor + # waiting*wait cost)	15.2667		
		Cost (Labor + # in system*wait cost)	17		

Cost vs. Servers _ □ X

Example 8: Costing Solution		
Number of servers	Total cost based on waiting	Total cost based on system
1	15.2667	17
2	8.4007	10.1341
3	12.0518	13.7851
4	16.007	17.7403
5	20.0009	21.7342

 # Work Measurement

This module can be used for the three major areas of work measurement: time study, computation of sample size for time study, and work sampling

Example 1: Time Study

A sample screen that includes the data appears next. The process consists of three elements and 5 observations of each element have been taken.

Allowance factor		.05	Instruction	Enter the name for this element. Almost any character is permissible.			

Example						
	Performance rating	Obs 1	Obs 2	Obs 3	Obs 4	Obs 5
Element 1	100	50	60	45	50	55
Element 2	90	25	0	24	25	29
Element 3	110	10	9	11	10	9

Data

Performance rating. For each element, its performance rating must be given. The normal time will be computed as the average time multiplied by the performance rating.

Observations. The time observed for each element must be entered. In some cases, observations will be bad (outliers). In order to exclude them from computations, enter a 0, as in the case of Observation 2 for Element 2.

Allowance factor. The overall allowance factor is given. This allowance factor adjusts the final time for the sum of all three normal times.

Solution

Following is the solution screen for the example.

Average. The average for each element is computed. Notice that the average for Elements 1 and 3 are taken over 5 values, but that the average for Element 2 is taken over 4 values because observation 2 was given as 0 and this is not included in the averaging process.

Standard deviation. The standard deviation for each element is computed, although it is not used for any further computations in this submodel.

Normal time. The normal time is computed by multiplying the average of the observations by the performance rating for that element.

Work measurement Results									
Example									
	Average	Sample Std dev	Normal	Performance rating	Obs 1	Obs 2	Obs 3	Obs 4	Obs 5
Element 1	52	5.7009	52	100	50	60	45	50	55
Element 2	25.75	2.2174	23.175	90	25		24	25	29
Element 3	9.8	.8367	10.78	110	10	9	11	10	9
Normal proc time			85.955						
Standard time			90.479						

Normal processing time. The normal processing time is the sum of the normal times.

Standard time. The standard time is computed in one of two ways depending on the textbook. Some authors use

standard time = normal processing time * (1 + allowance factor)

whereas others use:

standard time = normal processing time /(1 - allowance factor)

If you are using a Prentice Hall textbook the appropriate formula should be in use. If not, please check **Help, User Information** to be certain that the software is listed as using the correct textbook.

Example 2: Computing the sample size

Following is the data for the second example.

Confidence	Instruction
2 sigma (95.45%) ▼	Enter the value for element 1 for accuracy level. This is a probability or a percentage so it must be between 0 and 1.

	Accuracy level	Obs 1	Obs 2	Obs 3	Obs 4	Obs 5
Example 2						
Element 1	.05	50	60	45	50	55
Element 2	.01	25	0	24	25	29
Element 3	.1	10	9	11	10	9

The input is similar to the preceding time study above, but the goal is different. The goal is to find the minimum sample size to be 99.45 percent confident of our results. The input for this submodel is as follows:

Accuracy level. Within what percentage should the results hold? For example, for Element 2 there should be 95.45 percent confidence that our results are within 1 percent of the true time.

Observations. This is the same as above. The time observed for each element must be entered. In some cases, observations will be bad (outliers). In order to exclude them from computations, enter a 0, as in the case of Observation 2 for Element 2.

Confidence. Six options about the confidence level are presented in the drop-down box above the data.

The output appears as follows. The sample sizes for the three elements are 20, 297, and 3, respectively. Generally, this means that we use the largest and have 297 observations of each element.

Work measurement Results									
			Example 2						
	Average	Sample Std dev	Sample size	Accuracy level	Obs 1	Obs 2	Obs 3	Obs 4	Obs 5
Element 1	52	5.7009	20	.05	50	60	45	50	55
Element 2	25.75	2.2174	297	.01	25		24	25	29
Element 3	9.8	.8367	3	.1	10	9	11	10	9

Example 3: Work sampling

An example of both the input and output for work sampling appears next:

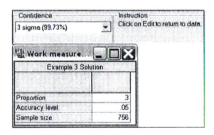

Proportion. This is the estimated proportion of time spent on the task.

Accuracy level. This is similar to the preceding accuracy level. Within what percentage should the results hold? For example, there should be 99.73 percent confidence that the results are within 5 percent of the true proportion.

Confidence. Six options about the confidence level are presented in the drop-down box above the data

The result is simply the sample size. In this case, we must sample 756 time units.

Appendices

Appendix A. Customization for Textbooks

Module	Customization
Decision analysis	Row names Hurwicz not included in all textbooks
Forecasting	Inclusion of Period 1 in error computation for exponential smoothing methods Computations for exponential smoothing with trend model varies by textbook
Inventory	EOQ with shortages model not included in all textbooks Safety stock model for normal distribution varies by textbook
Job shop scheduling	Method names Number of operations column not included in all textbooks
Linear programming	Simplex tableau display
Location	Model names
Materials requirements planning	Table display (order of rows)
Quality control	Acceptance sampling model not included in all textbooks
Simulation	Random number table
Waiting lines	Model availability and names Notation
Work measurement	Computation of standard time varies by textbook

Appendix B. Useful hints for modules

Module	Helpful Hints
Aggregate planning	This is a model where it may be useful to use the months as the row name option on the creation screen, rather than the default names of period 1, period 2, and so on. Also, the Copy down button is useful for entering constant capacities. In order to use the transportation submodel for aggregate planning, the costs can not vary from period to period. If the costs do vary, you must set up the model yourself using the transportation model.
Assembly-line balancing	Be sure the time unit for the tasks is set properly.
Assignment	Enter x to have a large cost (9,999) placed in the cell to preclude the assignment from being made.
Breakeven	For problems with two options and revenue simply treat revenue as a third option.
Decision tables	Use "=" in the probability row to set all probabilities to be equal for the decision tree. Note that in the one-period inventory model, the profits on excess units or shorted units can be negative, that is, a loss.
Forecasting	The standard error is computed using $n - 2$ in the denominator.
Integer and mixed integer programming	It is not necessary to include the non-negativity restrictions (e.g., $x >= 0$) when counting the number of constraints. The bottom left cell has a drop down box that can be used to set all variables to the same type.
Inventory	The holding cost in the EOQ based models can be entered as a number or as a percent. The entry .30 means 30 cents whereas the entry 30% means 30% of the unit cost.
Linear programming	It is not necessary to include the non-negativity restrictions (e.g., $x >= 0$) when counting the number of constraints. This is one of two modules where it is possible to step through the solution procedure.
MRP	Doubleclicking on the data table will display the MRP product tree. Also, the "Do not display 0s" button can be very useful in this module.
Quality	For control charts, you may use the average as the center line or set the center line yourself.

Statistics	This module includes a normal distribution calculation submodel. The same calculations can be performed with the normal distribution tool (toolbar or main menu TOOLS), which has a different (better) user interface.
Transportation	Enter x to have a large cost (9,999) placed in the cell to preclude units being shipped from the original location to the destination. This is one of two modules where it is possible to step through the solution procedure.
Waiting	Both arrivals and service are given by RATEs rather than TIMEs. Be sure that the time unit for the arrival rate and service rate are the same.

SITE LICENSE AGREEMENT AND LIMITED WARRANTY

READ THIS LICENSE CAREFULLY BEFORE USING THIS PACKAGE. BY USING THIS PACKAGE, YOU ARE AGREEING TO THE TERMS AND CONDITIONS OF THIS LICENSE. IF YOU DO NOT AGREE, DO NOT USE THE PACKAGE. PROMPTLY RETURN THE UNUSED PACKAGE AND ALL ACCOMPANYING ITEMS TO THE PLACE YOU OBTAINED. *THESE TERMS APPLY TO ALL LICENSED SOFTWARE ON THE DISK EXCEPT THAT THE TERMS FOR USE OF ANY SHAREWARE OR FREEWARE ON THE DISKETTES ARE AS SET FORTH IN THE ELECTRONIC LICENSE LOCATED ON THE DISK:*

1. GRANT OF LICENSE and OWNERSHIP: The enclosed computer programs and data ("Software") are licensed, not sold, to you by Prentice-Hall, Inc. ("We" or the "Company") in consideration of your purchase or adoption of the accompanying Company textbooks and/or other materials, and your agreement to these terms. We reserve any rights not granted to you. You own only the disk(s) but we and/or licensors own the Software itself. This license allows you to install, use, and display the enclosed copy of the Software on individual computers in the computer lab designated for use by any students of a course requiring the accompanying Company textbook and only for the as long as such textbook is a required text for such course, at a single campus or branch or geographic location of an educational institution, for academic use only, so long as you comply with the terms of this Agreement..

2. RESTRICTIONS: You may not transfer or distribute the Software or documentation to anyone else. Except for backup, you may not copy the documentation or the Software. You may not reverse engineer, disassemble, decompile, modify, adapt, translate, or create derivative works based on the Software or the Documentation. You may be held legally responsible for any copying or copyright infringement that is caused by your failure to abide by the terms of these restrictions.

3. TERMINATION: This license is effective until terminated. This license will terminate automatically without notice from the Company if you fail to comply with any provisions or limitations of this license. Upon termination, you shall destroy the Documentation and all copies of the Software. All provisions of this Agreement as to limitation and disclaimer of warranties, limitation of liability, remedies or damages, and our ownership rights shall survive termination.

4. LIMITED WARRANTY AND DISCLAIMER OF WARRANTY: Company warrants that for a period of 60 days from the date you purchase this Software (or purchase or adopt the accompanying textbook), the Software, when properly installed and used in accordance with the Documentation, will operate in substantial conformity with the description of the Software set forth in the Documentation, and that for a period of 30 days the disk(s) on which the Software is delivered shall be free from defects in materials and workmanship under normal use. The Company does not warrant that the Software will meet your requirements or that the operation of the Software will be uninterrupted or error-free. Your only remedy and the Company's only obligation under these limited warranties is, at the Company's option, return of the disk for a refund of any amounts paid for it by you or replacement of the disk. THIS LIMITED WARRANTY IS THE ONLY WARRANTY PROVIDED BY THE COMPANY AND ITS LICENSORS, AND THE COMPANY AND ITS LICENSORS DISCLAIM ALL OTHER WARRANTIES, EXPRESS OR IMPLIED, INCLUDING WITHOUT LIMITATION, THE IMPLIED WARRANTIES OF MERCHANTABILITY AND FITNESS FOR A PARTICULAR PURPOSE. THE COMPANY DOES NOT WARRANT, GUARANTEE OR MAKE ANY REPRESENTATION REGARDING THE ACCURACY, RELIABILITY, CURRENTNESS, USE, OR RESULTS OF USE, OF THE SOFTWARE.

5. LIMITATION OF REMEDIES AND DAMAGES: IN NO EVENT, SHALL THE COMPANY OR ITS EMPLOYEES, AGENTS, LICENSORS, OR CONTRACTORS BE LIABLE FOR ANY INCIDENTAL, INDIRECT, SPECIAL, OR CONSEQUENTIAL DAMAGES ARISING OUT OF OR IN CONNECTION WITH THIS LICENSE OR THE SOFTWARE, INCLUDING FOR LOSS OF USE, LOSS OF DATA, LOSS OF INCOME OR PROFIT, OR OTHER LOSSES, SUSTAINED AS A RESULT OF INJURY TO ANY PERSON, OR LOSS OF OR DAMAGE TO PROPERTY, OR CLAIMS OF THIRD PARTIES, EVEN IF THE COMPANY OR AN AUTHORIZED REPRESENTATIVE OF THE COMPANY HAS BEEN ADVISED OF THE POSSIBILITY OF SUCH DAMAGES. IN NO EVENT SHALL THE LIABILITY OF THE COMPANY FOR DAMAGES WITH RESPECT TO THE SOFTWARE EXCEED THE AMOUNTS ACTUALLY PAID BY YOU, IF ANY, FOR THE SOFTWARE OR THE ACCOMPANYING TEXTBOOK. SOME JURISDICTIONS DO NOT ALLOW THE LIMITATION OF LIABILITY IN CERTAIN CIRCUMSTANCES, THE ABOVE LIMITATIONS MAY NOT ALWAYS APPLY.

6. GENERAL: THIS AGREEMENT SHALL BE CONSTRUED IN ACCORDANCE WITH THE LAWS OF THE UNITED STATES OF AMERICA AND THE STATE OF NEW YORK, APPLICABLE TO CONTRACTS MADE IN NEW YORK, AND SHALL BENEFIT THE COMPANY, ITS AFFILIATES AND ASSIGNEES. This Agreement is the complete and exclusive statement of the agreement between you and the Company and supersedes all proposals, prior agreements, oral or written, and any other communications between you and the company or any of its representatives relating to the subject matter. If you are a U.S. Government user, this Software is licensed with "restricted rights" as set forth in subparagraphs (a)-(d) of the Commercial Computer-Restricted Rights clause at FAR 52.227-19 or in subparagraphs (c)(1)(ii) of the Rights in Technical Data and Computer Software clause at DFARS 252.227-7013, and similar clauses, as applicable.

Should you have any questions concerning this agreement or if you wish to contact the Company for any reason, please contact in writing: **Director, Media Production, Pearson Education, 1 Lake Street, Upper Saddle River, NJ 07458**